Endorsements for "Can I See Your Hands!"

A rarity in the security field, Gav Schneider blends comprehensive operational experience with a strategic, forward-looking approach towards ensuring that safety… in all forms… is at the forefront of individual and group decision making. The duality of his experiences, in the field and the halls of academia, enable Gav to provide credible, succinct, and actionable guidance to anyone interested in protecting themselves and creating safer environments.

– Claire S. Willette (former US Department of Defense Official; Senior Expert Advisor to the International Standards Risk and Security Committees; and Principal at Windrose International Pty Ltd, Strategic Policy and Risk Consultants.

"Can I see your hands" is the title and underpinning philosophy of this fascinating and very personal book by Dr Gavriel Schneider, focused on the issues of personal risk management, personal safety and personal resilience. As an emergency services leader, I understand how personal resilience is a key part of effective performance under pressure, and in my experience resilient individuals tend to be more adaptive and able to cope even in difficult times. Resilient individuals are also more likely to 'bounce back' in difficult times and this description also applies to martial arts training for example in learning to fall correctly (an essential skill in martial arts that is covered in the book) – and repeatedly picking yourself up and start all

over again. At one level this is a practical skill that simply improves personal safety, but is also a metaphor for bouncing back from situations that sometimes happen in life. This is just one of many examples of how the author uses his many, many years of martial arts training to give everyone some simple tools to improve their personal resilience safety and security.

The personal reflections and insight of the author give the reader a strong sense of the work and dedication the author has put in to perfecting his ability, and his very personal style allows the reader to establish a better attitude of awareness to protect your personal safety and improve your personal resilience to the risks we all face in our everyday lives.

– Tony McGuirk was former Chief Executive and Chief Fire Officer of Merseyside Fire and Rescue Service, one of the most complex emergency management organisations in the UK. He has been a National Adviser on Emergency Management in the UK, and has extensive experience of dealing with crises, emergencies and disasters. He was awarded the Queens Fire Service medal in 2006, and made a Commander of the British Empire in 2011. He has worked in North America, Canada, Europe and the UAE and in 2015 he moved to Australia having been awarded a Distinguished Talent visa for his work in disaster and emergency response and management. He is a Fellow of the International Institute of Risk and Safety Management, and a Fellow of the International Institution of Fire Engineers.

Gavriel Schneider has been a source of invaluable information and inspiration to me personally since my arrival in Johannesburg almost 10 years ago and during my transition into the private security sector. 'Can I see your hands!' builds on my learning and teaching as a police officer and a security consultant, as it emphasises the fundamental principles of crime prevention and personal safety – where prevention is the primary aim.

Gavriel's writing style is clear, and to the point, and gives a detailed understanding of the knowledge, skills and experience required for a proactive approach to personal risk management.

I recommend that everyone should read this book – as doing so will undoubtedly save lives!

- Dave Dodge – Dave was a London police officer for over 30 years and has been a safety and security consultant in Southern Africa for 10 years, much of this time involved in the provision of education and training to law enforcement officers and corporate clients. In addition to being an assessor and verifier for international security qualifications, he is an acknowledged expert on security risk assessments and the development and implementation of international standards. Dave is the Chairman of the South African Institute of Security and ASIS International, Chapter 155, Johannesburg.

Gav's personal insights and academic knowledge make this book a must for anyone who wants to think about their security and that of those they love. This book is useful for lots of different people!

- Jason L Brown – FSyI, CSyP, RSecP. National Security Director, Thales Australia & New Zealand. Chair of ISO/TC 262 Risk Management Technical Committee and Chairman of the Board of Security Professionals Australasia.

In today's fast paced world of change and constant connection, we are regularly reminded of the real and digital threats that surround us. In response, we cannot survive without the natural mental shortcuts we take; yet these seemingly beneficial shortcuts open the door to being taken advantage of, and can lead to potentially dangerous situations. Gav's book teaches us the importance of understanding these natural processes and reinforces the need to take personal responsibility in such situations. He provides a framework and practical steps each of us can take to improve our personal safety and that of our loved ones.

This book is a poignant reminder that as the world knocks on our front door, we need to be appropriately vigilant about who we let in.

- Tom Ristoski – Executive Director Strategic Partnerships & Executive Education at Australian Catholic University.

I have known Gavriel for more than 20 years. Since he was a young man, he worked to be one of the best students in Martial Arts. I taught and trained Gav, for a while and saw his values and persistence to achieve his goals. His dedication for pursuing his goals are noteworthy. Over the years, he continued his studies and developed to be a master in Martial Arts and achived his Doctorate, I am very proud of him, Gav grew and became a leading force in self-defense and Security Risk Management. I can proudly call him my Friend and a professional partner in self – defense and counter-terrorism.

- Yaron Hanover is a Grand Master black belt, he is a 10th Dan Professional martial artist, Krav Maga, MMA and international counter- terrorism Expert. He is the CEO of the Hanover tool box company which Manufactures innovative self-defense tools. He has dedicated his life in pursuing excellence in these fields, putting an emphasis on weapons training and knife fighting. Yaron has served and trained Israel's top military and government counter-terrorism units, as well as facilitated training for similar units around the world. Yaron has headed the personal security of such persons as Michael Jackson while on tour. Yaron holds many Israeli national champion titles and as a Senior instructor has a legacy of personally training well over 35,000 students. He holds certification as a 10th Dan Grand Master DSSJ, is featured on the Krav Maga Wall of Fame and has Master titles from the International Budo Association, as well as the European (EJJU), American, British and South African Jiu-Jitsu Association.

Dr Gav Schneider has written a must-read guide for anyone considering that it might be a good idea to know about protecting what counts in the many complex moments we must deal with in everyday life. Read this book and learn from one of the best – Can I See Your Hands is a rare insight into the mind of a true Master.

– Kate Down, Behavioural Scientist.

In a time when Global, Regional, Local, and personal safety appears to be on an ever-increasing cycle of decline, this book by Gav offers a congruence of his own personal journey, that has been a lifelong dedication to understanding the increasing threat environment and his commitment to sharing his extensive knowledge and experiences for the greater good of all. I commend Gav for his commitment and delivery of this personal and excellent read, that really demonstrates not only his commitment to "real life" experiences, and demonstrates an academic commitment that delivers a comprehensive and credible guideline that allows the reader to implement solutions to safety, with the confidence of his wealth of knowledge and legitimacy.

On a personal level, I commend Gav's commitment to personal integrity, resilience and the endless pursuit for growth and excellence, the traits I see he carries and delivers in all facets of his private and professional life.

– Mark Carrick: Former Commander of New South Wales Police Terrorism Intelligence as well as the former National Capability Advisor on Counterterrorism Intelligence to the Australian Government's National Counterterrorism Committee. Mark is one of Australia's most experienced Counter Terrorism practitioners, with over 20 years' experience in Law Enforcement spanning many disciplines including, Witness Protection, Close Personal Protection, Crime Management, Change Management and Counter Terrorism Intelligence. In 2010 Mark became the first Police Officer in

Australia to receive the rare ANZAC of the year award from the Australian Governor.

Gavriel Schneider has written a quintessential manuscript on self protective strategies. In today's society of ever increasing violence, it is no longer rational to solely rely on others for your wellbeing. This book provides a systematic approach to our daily routines to reduce the risk of becoming a victim, it enables us to effectively contribute to our own safety and that of our family

– Steve Furmedge: Director Security – Public Transport Western Australia and 8th Degree Black Belt.

"Risk" is a term that gets used often, but is seldom understood; we all think that we know what it means, however when we are asked to provide a definition we find ourselves unable to give one. Gavriel Schneider, is an expert at identifying, defining and determining risk, and providing means for reducing, mitigating and dealing with it. This book is a manual/textbook in risk management. If you have an interest in learning how to predict, identify, and avoid violence, this should be a book that is in your library.

– Gershon Ben Keren, 5th Degree Black Belt, Professional Security Consultant & Amazon Best Selling Author.

In today's often violent-ridden world, be it in public spaces or even the supposed safety of one's own home, this book is a timely reminder that people with intent can hurt and seriously injure or kill other people who are not prepared to defend themselves and/or protect loved ones. In a logical progression of practical steps Dr. Gavriel Schneider has outlined how to prepare oneself not only physically and mentally to either implement avoidance or deflecting mental strategies but also to be prepared to physically defend oneself (becoming a 'hard target'), particularly when there might be no-one else readily available or nearby to do the 'protecting' on your behalf. This book admirably accomplishes the initial aim as being "to create a base level of proactive awareness and preparedness that will empower" the individual in accomplishing self-protection as such situations might suddenly arise when one is in a vulnerable and unprotected position. In other words, it provides the individual with some skills to manage any threat with the objective of surviving such an incident with the minimum amount of injury or loss. By the nature of the book it deals with 'worst-case scenarios' as a way of mentally preparing (denial avoidance) and acceptance that the risks (probability) of 'bad things happening to good people' are a constant threat to ordinary people in today's unpredictable world. A recommended read for all interested in preparing for those violence risk possibilities and to be able to 'look after yourself' in any potentially violent and/or dangerous situation. The overall message of the book is clearly stated that, as individuals, we need to accept that we must take responsibility, to some degree, for our own safety and security.

Professor Anthony Minnaar
Research Professor of Criminal Justice Studies
University of South Africa

CAN I SEE YOUR HANDS!

CAN I SEE YOUR HANDS!

A Guide to Situational Awareness, Personal Risk Management, Resilience and Security

Dr. Gavriel (Gav) Schneider

CPP, FGIA, FAIM, FIS (SA), 7th Dan

Foreword by:

Dave Grossman

Lt. Colonel, US Army (ret.)

Author of: On Killing, On Combat, and Assassination Generation

Universal Publishers

Irvine • Boca Raton

Can I See Your Hands!
A Guide to Situational Awareness, Personal Risk Management,
Resilience and Security

Universal Publishers
Irvine • Boca Raton
USA • 2017
www.universal-publishers.com

978-1-62734-184-4 (pbk.)
978-1-62734-185-1 (ebk.)

Typeset by Medlar Publishing Solutions Pvt Ltd, India

Publisher's Cataloging-in-Publication Data

Names: Schneider, Gavriel.
Title: Can I see your hands : a guide to situational awareness, personal risk
    management, resilience and security / Dr. Gav Schneider.
Description: Irvine, CA : Universal Publishers, 2017.
Identifiers: LCCN 2017945503 | ISBN 978-1-62734-184-4 (pbk.) |
    ISBN 978-1-62734-185-1 (ebook)
Subjects: LCSH: Self-defense. | Risk perception. | Threats--Prevention. |
    Crime prevention. | Security (Psychology) | BISAC: REFERENCE /
    Personal & Practical Guides.
Classification: LCC HV7431 .S345 2017 (print) | LCC HV7431 (ebook) |
    DDC 613.6--dc23.

Dedication

*To all the brave men and women that take the initiative to
protect those who cannot protect themselves… and to those
who will make the hard decisions to do the right thing at the
right time in the future!*

*This book is dedicated to my mentor and friend, the late
Major David Sharp, your life experience, and knowledge is
well remembered – as you used to say:*

"Moving On Now"
Major (Ret) D.M. Sharp –
BEM. HM (P.F. ROK), Comm. M (USA)

"The Only Thing Necessary for the Triumph of Evil is that Good Men (or Women) Do Nothing"

Edmund Burke

Contents

Foreword

by Dave Grossman
– Lt. Colonel, US Army (ret.)

You hold in your hands an amazing book, unlike any other on the subject. Many good books have been written about the critically important topic of protecting yourself and your loved ones from violence. And the best of these, such as Gavin de Becker's The Gift of Fear, have been integrated and applied in this book.

Consider, just this one aspect of what Dr. Gav Schneider has done to make this the best possible book on this subject. You will find many books on many topics that seem to operate in a vacuum. But the best books on any subject are those that "stand on the shoulders of giants" and build on that which has already been written, skillfully weaving these together with new information and new insight, to create a book that is greater than the sum of its parts. And that is what Gav has done in this book, incorporating, applying, and recommending some of the great works that have been previously written on this vital subject.

The next factor that makes this book truly unique and important, is the incredibly thorough and comprehensive scope of (as Gav puts it) the "level of awareness, prevention and capability that the average, everyday person needs" to deal with the threats that face the average citizen today.

I have read many books on this subject, and I can honestly say that no one has come even close to matching Gav in addressing the full span of diverse challenges that face the average citizen today.

Finally, the author, Dr. Gav Schneider, is truly and uniquely qualified to write this book. Drawing upon his experiences in 17 nations, a leading academic and speaker, a Doctorate in Criminology and a 7th Degree Black Belt, just to cover a few of his qualifications.

He has "been there" and "done that." Most of all, Gav has had a lifetime of real-world experiences, which he applies in a powerful and masterful manner, in order to give you, the reader, a truly valuable and unique resource to face the dangers of an increasingly violent world.

And we have never needed this book more than we do now.

Wherever you are, right now, as you read these words, you can probably look up and see some of the things our society has done to prepare for the threat of fire. Some form of "fire code" has influenced the building you are in, right now. You can probably see smoke alarms and possibly fire-exit signs. A fire extinguisher or a fire hydrant may be directly in sight.

By some estimates, half the construction cost of a modern building will go into meeting the requirements of the "fire code". Fireproof or fire-retardant material for the structure of the building, and for internal furnishings, versus the cheapest alternative. Electrical system brought up to fire code. Double the electrical system in some buildings, to run wiring to all fire-exit signs and smoke alarms. Fire sprinkler system under pressure for the lifetime of the building.

The "fire alarm" in many buildings is an amazing expense all by itself, with a separate network of wiring, running through our civilization, from every building to the local fire station. And from our youngest days we did "fire drills" and perhaps you were taught "stop, drop and roll" in case you ever caught on fire.

Vast amounts of money, time and effort go into preparing for fire. In the United States, every year around 300 people are killed by fire, by approximately 15,000 are killed by violence. If we can spend all this money and time to prepare for fire (and we should) how much more so should we prepare for violence?

And yet, the comparison between fire and violence completely breaks down, when we consider the psychological effects of "natural factors" versus violence.

During the 9–11 attacks in the United States, terrorists murdered over 3,000 citizens. The stock market crashed, the US invaded two nations, and our world changed dramatically.

That same year, over 30,000 Americans were killed in traffic accidents, and it didn't change anything. Because they were accidents.

The Diagnostic and Statistical Manual of the American Psychiatric Association (the "Bible" of psychiatry and psychology) tells us that whenever the "cause" of a traumatic event is "human in nature" the degree of psychological trauma is "usually more severe and long lasting."

Ask yourself how you would respond to these two scenarios:

1. A tornado (or earthquake or fire or tsunami) hits your house while you are gone, and puts your whole family in the hospital. How do you feel about that?

   Most people would say that they are glad their family had survived.

2. A gang hits your house while you are gone, and beats your whole family into the hospital. How do you feel about that one?

   Most people do have to admit that there is a vast difference between the way these two scenarios make us feel. We have to admit to ourselves that preparation for violence is usually minimal if addressed at all…

Consider:

– The attack on the World Trade Center on September 11, 2001, with 2,996 dead. Generally considered the most horrendous terrorist attack in history.

– 69 murdered and 120 wounded on Utoya, Norway, in 2011, in the most horrendous massacre by a single individual with a firearm.

– 15 murdered by a student in Winnenden, Germany, 2009, in the worst massacre by a juvenile in history.

...This is not some ancient history. Not some distant land. This is us. Now.

In the US, the FBI tells us that the number of mass murders are doubling every decade, and the average body count is going up. And you do not have to go any further than the front page of your newspaper to find similar examples in your own part of the world.

There is a new twist to terrorism: It's called body count. Whether the perpetrators are school killers, workplace killers, or international terrorists, they are not interested in negotiating; their only goal is to kill as many people as humanly possible.

The defining challenge of the years to come is to protect our loved ones, our students, our customers, and our employees from violence, in the same way that we protect them from fire.

But wait. The sky is not falling. It is completely within our ability to meet this challenge. There are simple, straightforward measures we can take, to protect ourselves and our loved ones from violence.

And you hold in your hands the finest available guideline, by the most eminently qualified individual, uniquely designed to help you to meet this need. With all my heart, I encourage you to read, study and apply this book into your own life, to protect what is most dear and precious to us, to protect what counts.

Dave Grossman
Lt. Colonel, US Army (ret.)
Author of On Killing, On Combat,
and Assassination Generation
Director, Killology Research Group,
www.killology.com

About Dave Grossman

Lt. Col. Dave Grossman is a former West Point psychology professor, Professor of Military Science, and an Army Ranger who is the author of On Killing, On Combat, and Assassination Generation. Col. Grossman's work has been translated into many languages, and his books are required or recommended reading in colleges, military academies, and police academies around the world, these include the US Marine Corps Commandant's reading list and the FBI Academy reading list. His research, was cited by the President of the United States in a national address after the Littleton, Colorado school massacre, and he has testified before the US Senate, the US Congress, and numerous state legislatures. He has served as an expert witness and consultant in state and Federal courts, including the well-known UNITED STATES vs. TIMOTHY MCVEIGH.

He helped train mental health professionals after the Jonesboro school massacre, and he was also involved in counselling or court cases in the aftermath of the Paducah, Springfield, and Littleton school shootings. He has been called upon to write the entry on "Aggression and Violence" in the Oxford Companion to American Military History, three entries in the Academic Press Encyclopedia of Violence, Peace and Conflict and has presented papers before the national conventions of the American Medical Association, the American Psychiatric Association, the American Psychological Association, and the American Academy of Pediatrics. He also has published several novels, and he has five US patents to his name. He has a black belt in Hojutsu, the martial art of the firearm, and has been inducted into the USA Martial Arts Hall of Fame.

Today he is the director of the Killology Research Group (www.killology.com), and in the wake of the 9/11 terrorist attacks he has been on the road 250 days a year, training elite military and law enforcement organizations worldwide about the reality of combat, and he has written extensively on the terrorist threat with articles published in the Harvard Journal of Law and Public Policy and many leading law enforcement journals.

Preface

I t is hard to provide credit where credit is due to all who have influenced this work. This work is based on three decades of cumulative experience and consolidated, based on my own interpretation and experiences. I apologise in advance for missing out anyone or not giving respect or kudos where due. For where I have re-interpreted and adjusted other people's work based on my own experience of explaining and teaching, I have attempted not to overshadow or diminish the values of previous contributions and attempted to purposefully not revisit respective experts work in too much detail, whilst seeking to explain it in my own words.

I have tried to accurately recall past events when given as examples and have attempted to ensure, to the best of my ability, correctness. However, time and memory may have influenced my recall as it does for everyone.

Every attempt has been made to remain gender sensitive but in certain cases where terms are described in the male context, it has been done so based on simplicity and unless specifically specified, should be read as being gender inclusive or reciprocal i.e. he/she, his/her, etc. should be viewed as interchangeable.

In terms of political correctness and the tiny nuances that might cause people to take offence, please note that I have made every effort to be sensitive to issues that may cause concern. These days, however, it seems almost impossible to not offend someone. If you read this book and take offence to any aspects, please disregard them and move on to the next piece of information, as this may be something that could save your life and you do yourself a disservice by not persevering. I have worked, travelled, and/or trained in close to 20 countries and have enjoyed immersing myself in different cultures. As a white Jewish male, born in South Africa and now living in Australia, I have had great experiences with people of many cultures. I have been deployed protecting Arab Sheiks and Princes. I have had Black, Coloured, Indian, Asian, Christian, Muslim, Jew, and Hindu (and the occasional atheist), men and women work with me on protective teams or as my students from all over the world and, in every way, have quite literally placed my life in their hands. I have found that, those who complain the most about cultural sensitivity and gender issues are usually the ones who are not out there getting on with things. So, in the spirit of what this book is all about, I urge the reader to 'get on with things' and not try to interrogate the material in ways that do not add value.

This book is structured sequentially i.e. you need to read the chapters in order, However, the final section titled *Annexure: Scenarios and Applications*, can be applied as a standalone summary where the application of some of the principles and concept discussed in the book are applied to practical scenarios and examples.

For those of you in a rush there are key point Text Boxes and bolded text throughout which should enable you to be able to scan through the book and pick up some of the key concepts and principles. Or if you want a refresher – you can simply page through the book and review the Text Boxes, bolded texts, and chapter summaries.

Academic referencing has been applied in a very basic form to ensure credit is given where due however, to ensure a flowing and easy read, this has not followed standard academic referencing systems.

For more information on my companies online and face to face training please visit www.risk2solution.com

Acknowledgements

This work is an attempt to distil and summarize two decades of exposure and experience in terms of the risk management, martial arts, safety, and security industries along with striving to live a life of integrity. Indeed, every influence, both positive and negative, has contributed to the compilation of the contents of this book. Listing all influences would be a book in itself. However, I would like to start off thanking my grandfather – Sonny Cooper who has exemplified what it means to be a role model and how to live a life of dignity and respect. My wife, who is a constant base of support and my kids who have reminded me how important it is to play. My parents who have continued to support and encourage me, no matter how far apart we have been at times. A special note to my father for his excellent editing work. My siblings who are over achievers in their own right. Dr. Dennis Hanover, Master Vernon Rosenberg, GM Yaron Hanover, GM Guy Hanover and all of my other teachers, mentors and friends whose knowledge and guidance is beyond value. To the contributors of knowledge in their fields, Dave Grossman, Geoff Thompson, Gavin de Becker, and numerous others whose work in this area and whose publications are incredibly valuable in empowering people to lead healthier and safer lives. To Professor Anthony Minnaar – a true academic Superman. Special thanks to Marc Botes for his contributions and assistance with editing and formatting. To Mac McGuire who exemplifies 'the never give up spirit'; to my fellow warriors at Gendai Ryu and the Modern Warrior Alliance, my colleagues and partners at Risk 2 Solution and to the the police officers, soldiers, security professionals, martial artists and everyday people, who when the time is required, have unleashed their inner sheepdog and with whom I have had the honor of working with over the years – thank you for your continued professionalism towards keeping people safe and making sure that there is a base for good in this world.

Lastly, thank you to you, the reader, who by taking the time to read this book and apply some of its contents, is directly contributing to making the world a safer place for all of us.

About This Book

The title of this book: CAN I SEE YOUR HANDS! Refers to one of the key outcomes of this book – being able to tell if people want to cause us harm or not. In a very simplistic form, if you can see someone's hands and they are not concealing them, holding a weapon, or positioning to strike you, our levels of trust and confidence can increase. This simple example can serve as a reminder for us in many of the complex moments we must deal with in everyday life. The complexities and threats of our fast paced and modern world have never been more diverse or challenging than they are now, ranging from ever evolving cybercrime, modern day terrorism to old fashioned violent assault and petty crime. In addition, the fast-paced world, and the way we live bring levels of stress and pressure that our ancestors did not have to deal with, as an example the fact that we are now expected to be plugged in and reachable 24/7 in itself has many negative consequences from a health perspective. The aim of this book is to provide the reader with an understanding of how the world has changed in terms of the level of awareness, prevention and capability that the average, everyday person needs to consider towards keeping themselves and their loved one's safe. **This book is all about you**, the reader. The focus on you, the reader, is crucial because at the end of the day it doesn't really matter how skilled, competent or capable people like me are. The reality is that when things go wrong, those who, by definition are tasked to protect you, would probably not be there to assist. These include security officers, soldiers or law enforcement officers. Had they been present, the incident would probably not even have occurred.

The main aim of this book is to create a base level of proactive awareness and preparedness that will empower you, the reader, to enjoy your everyday life to the fullest. However, this freedom does come at a cost...

The world has changed in terms of how terrorists and criminals think and act. While technology and global travel have made things a lot easier and simpler for us, the core reality is that our opposition use these very same tools against us every day. Issues such as self-radicalized violent extremism, the evolution (or devolution) in terrorist methods of attack – from well-planned, complex and integrated attacks on targets of significance to lone-wolf attacks using simplistic weapons such as knives – have become commonplace. This has resulted in the normal civilian having to invest a significant amount of effort in personal safety and security. This is especially true in the western world, although far more individuals are killed by radicalized terrorists in areas like the Middle East or Africa than the media tends to report and focus on.

Despite the media's ongoing sensationalist broadcasting of global terrorist or criminal incidents, it is imperative that we maintain a sense of perspective when it comes to these issues. The fact is that globally, there are significant losses in numerous other areas (which actually makes terrorism in terms of loss of life and financial loss seem inconsequential) as well. Some of these include:

- Health and safety issues, including accidents in the workplace
- Medical issues
- Workplace violence
- Domestic violence
- Crime such as fraud, assault, and other related activities; etc.

In support of the above, the findings of a report compiled by the International Labour Organisation[1] entitled: "The cost of violence/stress

---

[1] *Source: Hoel, H, Sparks, K & Cooper, C (2001). The cost of violence/stress at work and the benefits of a violence/stress-free working environment.* Geneva: International Labor Organization (ILO).

at work and the benefits of a violence/stress-free working environment"
indicate some worrying issues[2]:

- *Violence (from external threats like terrorist attacks as well as internal threats) represents a problem in a growing number of workplaces even though the number exposed directly to physical assault remains relatively low. Employees in service industries, e.g. retailing and health care are most at risk of physical assaults whilst taxi-drivers and police officers are the most vulnerable groups with respect to homicide and, as has been demonstrated most recently, media institutions and those covered by the media are most vulnerable to terror attacks.*

- *Whilst violent attacks and even murders have received considerable attention in the US, across the world, a far greater number of people generally report being exposed to violence of a psychological nature (such as arises from publicised terror attacks) or bullying.*

- *The costs to organisations are primarily related to sickness, absenteeism, reduced productivity, replacement costs and additional retirement costs. A significant proportion of the workforce also report being exposed to sexual harassment. There may be further costs due to damage in production or equipment as well as costs in connection with grievance and litigation, e.g. investigation and mediation costs. A potential public loss of goodwill towards the organisation may be another more intangible cost.*

- *The costs to society are related to medical costs and possible hospitalisation, benefits and welfare costs in connection with premature retirement as well as potential loss of productive workers. On the basis of figures from a number of countries we estimate that in total, stress and violence at work may account for 1–3.5% of GDP.*

The goal is not really to divide threat issues into different categories as this can become very complicated in terms of having to have a

---

[2] *While this report seems to be a bit outdated the data and findings are certainly real and will most likely continue to be issues of concern for the foreseeable future.*

separate approach to terrorism, natural threats, crime, and other issues. The main goal is to basically establish an attitude of proactive awareness and some standard operating procedures (S.O.P.), or plans of action, that the individual can then take and superimpose onto his or her environment. The reasoning behind this is to provide the individual with the ability to identify, predict and hopefully avoid any threat that may cause them harm. Should it come to a worst-case scenario, where the threat cannot be avoided, our goal is to empower the individual with some skills to manage the threat with the objective of surviving such an incident with the minimum amount of injury or loss. Ideally, such skills would also extend to helping the individual's loved ones, or those around them. These skills should be integrated into the individual's everyday repertoire, and great care has been taken in this book to make these skills and tools as simplistic as possible. The reason for this is simple, the more complicated the skill, tool or SOP, the greater the chance that the individual will not be able to recall it in situations of extreme stress, and the more things can go wrong. The old adage "Keep It Simple, Stupid" (the 'KISS' principle) certainly holds true here.

> THE GOAL IS TO EMPOWER YOURSELF TO DEAL WITH WORST CASE SCENARIOS AND ELIMINATE DENIAL SO THAT WHEN FACING AN EXTREME SITUATION, YOU WILL KNOW WHAT TO DO. THE FIRST STEP IN ACHIEVING THIS IS SIMPLY ACCEPTING THAT SOMETIMES BAD THINGS HAPPEN TO GOOD PEOPLE.

The message is very simple – **we need to accept that we must take responsibility, to some degree, for our own safety and security.** Despite their best intentions, the authorities are fighting an intense, seemingly losing battle against extremism, cyber-crime, crime and evolving threats, simply because of the limited resources available to counter these threats. The goal is for you, the individual, to become part of the solution. This may mean you taking a more active role in contributing to your country, your region, your town and your neighborhood's specific security or safety setup. The aim is to not only make you, but also the community you live in, a more unattractive target for those who wish to harm others.

Accepting that something bad may happen to us is no easy matter, especially when that something bad may include losing our lives or the lives of loved ones, etc. And yet these are the very things we need to invest time and effort into, as unpleasant as it may be. As human beings, we are wired to ignore unpalatable issues, we believe that crime or terrorist attacks won't happen to us, and if it has happened before, that it can't possibly happen again. The goal of this book is one of empowerment. In my experience, I have found that people fear most that which they do not understand. With that in mind, this book will attempt to demystify how crimes and terrorist attacks are committed, and how we could proactively act to minimize these threats happening to us. The first step in this process is to accept that it could happen to you. Depending on where you live and what you have been exposed to in your life, this could be very easy or very difficult to do… It is crucial that we deal, once and for all, with the denial most of us harbor that somehow, we are exempt from these criminal activities and bad things happening to us.

From a psychological perspective, the well-known and often quoted 'Hierarchy of Needs' developed by the renowned Psychologist Abraham Maslow first published in 1943 in his paper "A theory of human motivation"[3] illustrates that we need to address our safety and security needs (bottom 2 levels) first before we can move onto other aspects. **As such this book is focused primarily on those aspects first, in order to form the foundational building blocks for more evolved needs that sit in the Self-Actualization level.** This is critically important, as I have found that whilst in today's modern world, where we often have the luxury to focus on the upper three levels of the pyramid

---

[3]Maslow, A.H. (1943). "A theory of human motivation". *Psychological Review*. 50(4): 370–96.

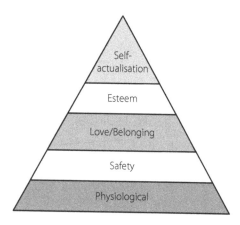

(Love/Belonging, Esteem and Self-Actualization) we tend to simply take for granted that our lower two foundational levels will always be met.

Thanks to many aspects such as the formalization of society, modern technology, etc. in most first world countries these aspects do seem to be a mandatory expectation. However, one simply must look at local crime statistics, chat to local law enforcement, ambulance, or emergency services officers, or notice the poor or unemployed in our communities and you realize that in many cases the expectation is not always met. Because of our inherent denial of unpalatable issues, we tend to keep blinkers on and not address the lower two levels of need in a coherent and structured manner, that is until something negative happens which forces action and skills development at these levels. In reality, our approach to self-development should be based on a solid foundation of knowing that we can address and manage our needs in the lower two levels and not rely on the uninformed perception that these levels will always be met because we expect that others manage them for us. As such, a focus on health and wellbeing, and safety and security are the key aspects of this book. The aim is to build a strong foundation of lower level knowledge, skills, and capabilities so that you can focus on the higher levels unencumbered by doubts and be prepared to deal with any issues that life may present. **A strong foundation is always the best way to build!**

The objective of this book is to create a base of knowledge and understanding, together with providing you with the skill sets you need to ensure that it's not just about surviving – it's about thriving. It's about being able to live your life the way you want to, in a safe manner. In many cases this level of enjoyment cannot be attained because of the blinkers we have on, in many cases without even knowing that we have them. This is especially true when we consider our own cognitive biases and related mental shortcuts[4] we have developed to cope with our complex world. In practical terms because of our biases and mental shortcuts, we experience a lack of awareness and become easy targets for people with ill intent. We can no longer apply what's known as the *ostrich syndrome*, where we stick our heads in the sand and hope that everything around us won't go wrong. And if it does, that it will become someone else's problem. We need to ensure that we have the capability to take the necessary actions when called for so that we become a key role player in ensuring that our world is a safer place, not just for us, but for our children too.

Action does not nec-
essarily mean that you
must become an expert
in self-defense and com-
bative skills. While learning to defend yourself is
a valid life skill, and one I
believe every person should
develop, the reality is that
developing just a few key
abilities can result in a

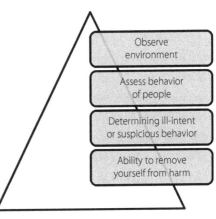

direct enhancement of your own and everyone's safety and wellbeing. These abilities start with self-knowledge and situational awareness and include some of the following:

The ability to observe your surroundings; the ability to evaluate and understand what may cause harm or be a threat; the ability to assess the behavior of the people around you; the ability to determine whether

---

[4]In order to understand these biases I strongly recommend reading the work of Daniel Kahneman and Dan Ariely – see the Bibliography & References Section for more information.

there is any ill intent or anything suspicious or out of the ordinary; and the ability to have the knowledge, foresight and confidence to remove yourself from such situations or in the worst case manage incidents if they occur. As well as the ability to report what you have noticed or experienced to the relevant authorities and finally and possibly the most important, is to maintain a robust mental state of resilience and be able to bounce back from things as required. The above skills can make a massive difference toward the well-being, safety and security of not only yourself, but all those around you.

Our goal should be to invest our effort and energy into the avoidance and prevention of situations that might cause harm or damage. This is directly opposed to focusing solely on survival and reaction – both of which remain critical skill sets but are reactive in nature. The reality is that if we allow situations that might cause harm to escalate to a point where we have to rely on these critical skill sets, our chances of walking away from such situations unscathed are slim to none. The essential point is that we all have a responsibility to work towards a safer and better world. **My objective with this book is to create a base platform for the reader to provide you with the knowledge that security and risk professionals have gained after many years of training and experience and all too often, take for granted that everyone possesses these skills**. This book strives to make the skills and knowledge available and accessible to everybody so that everybody can potentially switch themselves on when necessary and become active contributors to a safer world.

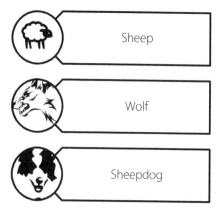

Dave Grossman, well-known author and researcher, presents a conceptual view of people today where he subdivides society into three main roles, namely sheep, wolves and sheepdogs.

THE PREMISE OF THIS BOOK IS FOR YOU TO FIND YOUR INNER PROTECTIVE CAPABILITIES (REFERRED TO AS SHEEPDOG CHARACTERISTICS). SO THAT IN A WORST-CASE SCENARIO YOU CAN PROTECT YOURSELF AND YOUR LOVED ONES!

The sheep is the person going about their everyday life, not wanting to be hassled or inconvenienced by security and safety concerns. Their safety and the safety and wellbeing of those around them is generally not a primary concern of the sheep. The second role is that of wolves, who prey on the sheep due to opportunities or their own sociopathic or psychopathic tendencies. Although there is no doubt that there are some really evil people in this world, in many cases these wolves may not have direct nefarious intent. Some are preying on the sheep based on their circumstances, such as criminals who justify their actions based on need and risk (i.e. stealing to eat). It should be noted, however, that no matter how 'noble' their reasons for preying on sheep are, they may still cause significant harm to the sheep. Some examples of clearly defined wolves are terrorists or career criminals. In many cases, Criminologists have found that in their own heads wolves may have justified that what they're doing is right from a psychological, ideological or religious perspective – even if it means blowing up a school bus full of children... No matter how these wolves rationalize their actions, from our perspectives their justifications can never validate them harming other people in pursuit of their ideology.

Lastly there are the sheepdogs. Sheepdogs protect the sheep from the wolves. Generally speaking, sheep don't like sheepdogs because they look like wolves. However, when the wolf comes knocking, the sheepdog is often valued above all else. The premise of this book is for you to find that little sheepdog inside yourself. The sheepdogs who have made a career out of protecting the sheep, such as those in the military, law-enforcement and related agencies, cannot be everywhere at the same time. Because wolves are cunning, chances are that when you are confronted with a wolf, those who are traditionally looked at as the sheepdogs may not be there to rescue you or your loved ones. Whilst you might tend to think of releasing your "inner sheepdog" only in violent situations, such as an armed robbery, assault with the intent of doing grievous bodily harm, etc. These are not necessarily the only situations that might require your inner sheepdog to be released. Think of situations like a fire breaking out in your home, being involved in a motor vehicle accident, or a child drowning in a swimming pool. All of these situations will require you to dig deep, and find the inner resolve to help those in need under immense pressure.

Another example may be basic cyber security. You might invest in the very best virus protection, firewalls and various other tools for your devices, but if you click on suspicious email links sent from an unknown source, *even if it is from your mysterious wealthy uncle living abroad, who would like to give you a million-dollar inheritance*, you may land up infecting and disabling your entire machine. In other words, spending money on protection is not beneficial if we do not apply an integrated approach and simply believe that because we have taken basic measures we are no longer at risk at all.

THE BASE LEVEL OF BEING A SHEEPDOG IS TAKING RESPONSIBILITY FOR YOUR OWN SAFETY AND SECURITY AND THAT OF PEOPLE AROUND YOU. LEARNING TO RELEASE YOUR INNER SHEEPDOG IS THE FUNDAMENTAL SHIFT THAT THIS BOOK IS ALL ABOUT!

A fundamental shift is required to first, identify and acknowledge the sheepdog in you (even if you are diametrically opposed to violence), and secondly to release it as and when needed. This is the foundational purpose of this book. It's imperative that you make the shift from relying on others to protect you and your loved ones to accepting that responsibility for yourself. We are very aware of the fact that the balance of being more aware of your surroundings, if unchecked can lean towards being paranoid. **Being paranoid is just as ineffective as not being aware at all. The goal is to enjoy life to the full whilst at the same time being more aware of what's going on around you.** I believe that the one cannot exist without the other, i.e. you can't truly squeeze the most out of life if you are paranoid or unaware. This book will attempt to assist you in this regard but you will have to find and continually adjust the balance for yourself. We call this balancing act Dynamic Risk Equilibrium (DRE). Living in fear of what "the wolves" might do and allowing that fear to dominate your life, actually translates to the wolves winning. It's crucial that you find a healthy balance between being prepared and enjoying life. The

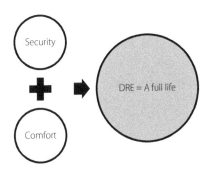

following simplistic diagram of the **Dynamic Risk Equilibrium (DRE)** may help you find this balance. We can interpret the diagram as follows:

The more security aware you are; the more comfort you sacrifice. Or alternatively, the more you cling to your comforts (e.g. taking a shortcut home, even though the shortcut leads through a dodgy part of town), the more you sacrifice on security. Both have a direct effect on you living a full life.

The more security awareness and balance you establish in your life and the lives of your loved ones, the more you will achieve comfort in the process. The converse is also true. The more you cling to your creature comforts at the expense of you and your loved ones' safety and security, the more your ability to live a life marked by relative safety and fulfillment will suffer. Only you can make the decision on what your ideal balance will be. It is important to remember too that as the name highlights DRE is dynamic and needs to be monitored and adjusted all the time.

Acronyms and Key Terms

- 3PC-S – Three Point Check System
- ARM – Adrenal Response management
- Awareness Tool Box – The set of tools which enable us to be aware and observant without being paranoid.
- Base Lining – the process of determining what is normal so we can identify what is not normal or suspicious.
- BDA – Before, During and After
- COI – Capability, Opportunity and Intent
- CPR – Cardio Pulmonary Resuscitation
- DDDRR – Detect, Deter, Delay, Respond and Recover
- DRE – Dynamic Risk Equilibrium
- ICE – Intercept, Control and Escape
- OODA – Observe, Orientate, Decide and Act
- PIAs – Planned Incident Actions
- PINS – Pre-incident Indicators
- PPRR – Plan, Prepare, Respond and Recover
- RHFC – Run, Hide, Fight and Communicate
- SOP – Standard Operating Procedure
- WoPM – Whole of Person Model

CHAPTER 1

Foundations

Why this book

Thank you for taking the time and energy to read this book. I congratulate you on taking the initiative to ensure that you grow your knowledge and skills or enhance your existing skill sets, to improve your quality of life and enhance your resilience capabilities. This will be achieved by learning how to embrace your natural instincts and focus on eliminating negative fears and perceptions which often bombard us. The core concept of what I am striving to achieve with this book is to provide you, the reader, with the base knowledge that specialist risk, security and associated professionals apply, in a simplistic and practical manner.

I have found, based on the experience I've accumulated in my career stretching over two decades thus far, that it is very important to learn how to live with, manage, and overcome fear and negative perceptions. This insight was gained by training *thousands of everyday people in personal security awareness and self-defense; training law-enforcement personnel, soldiers and security specialists, protecting presidents, celebrities and high net worth individuals, as well as providing advice to governments and major corporations.* The starting point to achieve this means not denying or avoiding issues but learning to understand and overcome these issues and threats which modern day life presents. As Nelson Mandela said:

> *"The brave man is not he who does not feel afraid,*
> *but he who conquers that fear."*

Experts such as Geoff Thompson, who has written many books on the topic, and Gavin de Becker, whose book 'The Gift of Fear' goes a long way to teaching people about intuition and how we should trust our inner voice. Such books are very useful and recommended sources (please see recommended reading section at the end of this book for a full list). One of the things that we have to remember is that fear itself is a survival response, triggered by our subconscious, based on information and stimuli collected from our surroundings. Inevitably, fear triggers our flight and fight response and in extreme circumstances could trigger our associated freeze or panic responses. **A core point that we need to remember is that fear, in itself, which triggers our fight and flight responses, has for thousands of years kept our ancestors safe and helped to keep our species alive. However, what is important for us in today's modern era, with its abounding complexities, is to ensure that we manage fear effectively so that we can have the quality of life we want.** This means we need to have the ability to sort through the information and stimuli that we are bombarded with every day and understand what's real and what's not real from a threat and associated action perspective.

Knowing real fear is quite a different reality to believing that something may go wrong or watching the television and having some sort of panic or fear response. I grew up in South Africa during the apartheid era, which was a period filled with violence, uncertainty and fear, and those who were there know that the situation was exceptionally volatile. My first self-defense instructor was a gentlemen by the name of Vernon Rosenberg who was an active police officer and an acknowledged innovator of practical combat systems. He was my primary instructor from ages 10–15 years old and he truly had me believing that attack was not only imminent but highly likely and could be coming at any time. This was something that led to a bit of paranoia on my side and in many cases led to me being overly prepared and not necessarily enjoying everything that I could during my teenage years. Despite this paranoia, falling asleep with gunshots in the background was a common reality and one we all became accustomed to as we lived in an area not far from one of the major township locations, Alexandra in Johannesburg (referred to colloquially as Alex). *As a side note – our charity (the Take Action Foundation) has run several successful development and upliftment projects in the same location of which we are very proud.* As a child, I was very sickly and there were certain doctors who said I would never be able to exercise my entire life. Fortunately, I got into martial arts at a young age and was able to go from strength to strength. It wasn't always easy and there were many, many challenges, but by the time I finished high school and had spent a year travelling around the world training with numerous well known martial arts masters, I had two second degree black belts in different systems and a first-degree black belt in a third system. I was an established member of the South African Taekwondo team and had been involved in numerous high level international competitions and actually started running my own martial arts school at the age of 14.

One of the first contracts I secured after returning from a year of travelling abroad and training was training bodyguard companies and specialist security operators. In exchange for doing their self-defense and unarmed combat training courses, I undertook all their close protection training. After about a year of training in these areas, when I had qualified in all the various skillsets, I commenced working as a professional bodyguard. It was a very interesting and challenging period and it was fraught with many challenges, where in many cases, dealing with male egos and actually physically proving what I was teaching, was a regular occurrence. This led to very early lessons in how to put bullies in their place and how to understand ways to motivate and empower other people.

Whilst the stories and examples of fear and related learnings are plentiful, let me share a quick anecdote. One night around the mid-1990s, before undergoing comprehensive bodyguard training, I was lying in bed about to fall asleep while living in South Africa, I heard a noise. It sounded like a riot across the street. As mentioned, we lived in an area that was not far from a township location where much of the violence was occurring. Thankfully, I was home alone at the time so I grabbed my firearm and a torch and I went to look over the wall and hearing the noise which sounded like close to 100 men screaming and shouting but could not see anything. I could hear gunshot sounds but because it was night and sound travels, judging distance is not easy and I could not tell how close the actual threat was. Police were on their way to respond; you could hear the sirens coming. However, realizing that they may take some time to arrive, I went back inside and went to retrieve additional ammunition just in case... I remember thinking to myself, I don't have time to run and I don't have enough ammunition if everybody jumps over the wall. What am I going to do?

I sat there that night and really considered the realities of having a plan and having a helpful, proactive response. From that time, while I already had a dedicated background in martial arts, I believed that there was a need to develop better skills and apply more effort to the way that I was able to respond and plan, to eliminate that fear of what would I do if the worst case happens and enable myself to act in an appropriate and effective manner.

Another key influencing event occurred several years later, still in South Africa. This event was a further trigger point for my search and journey into empowering, advising and educating people to be safer. Indeed, this event was a changing point and unfortunately sometimes, in order to learn big lessons, we must be willing to pay big prices. The event I am describing was the murder of my late stepfather, David Larsen in the late 1990s. Whilst my father had been held at gunpoint on several occasions he seemed to have handled these events well and I was quite young so it did not directly trigger the sheepdog response in me. However, at the time of my stepfather's murder, I was 21 years old, a professional martial arts instructor, a trained bodyguard spending my time between teaching self-defense, providing close protection and my academic and business studies. It would be fair to say that tactically I was on the top of my game. One Sunday evening around 9:30 pm, the telephone rang and it was my mother. She was on the way to the hospital with my stepfather who had just been shot in the head in an attempted vehicle carjacking as they were leaving their house in Johannesburg.

My immediate response was to grab my 'go-bag' and kit, which included items such as a firearm, spare magazines, knife, pepper spray, tactical torch and various other tools which were readily available (and legal in South Africa), and rush to the hospital. When I arrived at the hospital, I realized there was nothing I could do to assist and quickly went to the scene of the attack (outside my mother's house) to try and see what I could do there. When I got to the scene, I almost ended up having a shootout with what turned out to be two plain clothes policemen, who claimed that they were investigating the crime scene. From my perspective, all I saw were two men with their heads in the car helping themselves to whatever items they could locate of value and to this day, I believe they were more intent on stealing whatever was left in the vehicle than actually investigating the shooting. I had drawn my firearm and had it pointed at them before they were able to draw and point at me. It was one of those very tense and emotive times which literally, could have meant life or death. I'm very grateful to this day that I had received very good training in terms of properly assessing situations before making critical decisions (even under intense stress, when it counts the most) as thankfully no shots were fired.

In the madness and panic of that night, where it turned out that the bullet that killed my stepfather penetrated the headrest and only missed my mother's head by roughly an inch or two, it dawned on me that it truly didn't matter how skilled, competent, capable or effective I became as a fighter and protector, if I could not protect those who needed it when they needed it! It instilled in me a deep-seated interest in developing and understanding personal safety and security and learning how to share critical knowledge in such a way that I could pass that understanding on, in an effective manner.

Since forming my own business in 2001, we have trained thousands of people in close to 20 countries, in at least one of our personal safety, security awareness and related programs. We have been credited thousands of times with saving lives based on the knowledge and skills we have provided. The techniques and methodologies outlined in this book have been developed over many years, modified, adjusted, validated and applied by thousands of people successfully. However, it does not actually matter how many others have used the knowledge, **the key to benefitting from all the knowledge and information in this book is to make it your own**. If it doesn't make sense in the way I have explained it, if the words that I've used don't resonate with you, feel free to change and modify as you see fit so that it does makes sense to you. Adapt the contents and systems to concepts and principles that you may better understand and apply them as you see fit because the real truth is – **it is all about you. If you ever land up in a situation where something terrible happens to you or a loved one – wouldn't you like to have the knowledge and understanding to protect yourself and those you love? If so, you have picked up the right book… read on.**

Building a base of understanding

A base starting point in the journey of becoming a switched on and ready member of society is knowing how to ensure that we do not become victims. The core concept of this is understanding why people become victims in the first place. We tend to believe that because the vast majority of us grew up in societies that engender a respect for the rule of law, respect for people's physical existence and human rights that we therefore have a clear conviction of what is right and wrong. We somehow,

> WE HAVE FOUND THAT A PROACTIVE APPROACH CAN REDUCE THE LIKELIHOOD OF EXPOSURE TO VIOLENCE AND CRIME BY UP TO 90% – THAT'S A PRETTY GOOD ODD IN YOUR FAVOUR!

through a process of transference, instantly assume that everybody else should have the same paradigm, and if they don't, they're wrong.

The harsh reality is who, whether right or wrong, there are many people out there who don't have the same moral and judicial respect values that we believe all people should have. We therefore have to understand that sometimes bad things do happen to good people and that there are people in this world who would kill you for your watch or money or even because they believe that their religion is right and yours is wrong. Whilst it is a noble cause to drive human rights education and morals to try and achieve a global minimum standard, in my experience we have a long way to go…

Over the last two decades of training thousands of people and protecting some very exposed people, experience has shown us that in probably 90% of situations, harmful situations could have been avoided or even prevented from happening at all. In most cases, all that was needed was a proactive approach which focused on thinking and planning ahead, as well as taking the relevant steps to make the victim a hard and unattractive target to people who would cause them harm. We have found that there are roughly 5% of situations which we often refer to as 'the wrong time, wrong place' situations, where no matter how well you prepare, you may be caught in something that is out of your control. The other 5% are attacks or situations perpetrated by highly trained professionals which may be very hard to avoid and/or prevent and where no matter who you are or what you've done, you may be targeted. However, a 90% chance and probability of avoiding something negative happening to you, is a very good odd.

If we are truly capable of predicting bad things that could happen and then are able to take the steps to prevent them from happening, why is it that so many people get caught up in negative situations? We have found that generally there are a few reasons for this. The very first one is ignorance. People don't like to talk about things that involve safety and security because it means we have to look and consider the worst parts of human behavior and psychology. We have to consider all the negative and bad things that may happen to us and we have to accept that there are people out there who would perpetrate these bad things. As a result, we tend to avoid thinking about it all because it's uncomfortable to do so and thus we remain disempowered in being able to minimize the likelihood of our worst fears occurring.

Leading on from ignorance, the next big reason people become victims is negligence, where we actually do know better, or, we do know what we should do, yet we tend to just be lazy or we honestly believe that these negative things won't happen to us. By interviewing many people over the years, we have discovered that it's usually a combination of ignorance mixed with negligence and a healthy dose of denial that makes people the most attractive targets.

> WE NEED TO STRIVE TO ELIMINATE DENIAL, IGNORANCE, AND NEGLIGENCE SO WE CAN PREPARE PROPERLY AND MODIFY NEGATIVE BEHAVIOURS THAT MAKE US VULNERABLE...

Many years ago in South Africa, we had a woman who phoned our office and wanted to attend one of our "Vehicle Hijack Avoidance" training courses. Talking to her on the phone and assessing her motivation for wanting the training, she admitted that she had already been hijacked four times. Enquiring further, we asked how she was hijacked and how the attacks happened. To which she responded, "Ohhh, they hid behind the same bush every single time." Amazingly she had not realized that by not making any changes, she remained an attractive target, hence the multiple incidents. At no cost to her, we advised her to cut the bush and possibly install some lighting. When we asked her why, if she had experienced the same method of attack every time, she hadn't changed her behavior, she simply said that she did not think it would happen again and that "these things don't normally happen to people more than once…". As such she could not believe it would happen again but was now very worried. As you can see, this was a significant dose of ignorance – not understanding how attacks happen; negligence – not taking base measures to remove the likelihood of the event occurring again; as well as a healthy (I should say unhealthy) dose of denial by believing that after each incident, it would not happen again…

Let's define some of the words we've been talking about:

- **IGNORANCE** – "The condition of being *uninformed* or *uneducated*. A lack of knowledge or information." Synonyms – *unawareness/ blindness.*"
- **NEGLIGENCE** – "*Careless*, without appropriate or sufficient attention."
- **DENIAL** – "A *defense mechanism* involving a refusal to accept the truth of a phenomenon or prospect."

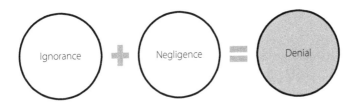

The reality is a combination of ignorance and negligence usually equals denial. We have this thought process of denial where if something bad has happened, we believe it won't happen again or we just plainly think that only bad things will happen to other people and not to us. We often don't take the measures required to ensure bad things won't happen to us. In fact, the converse is absolutely true, if you have been a victim before, you actually may be more likely to be a victim again, unless you alter your behavior. The reason is because the very characteristics that made a criminal select you as their victim initially would be repeated and therefore be attractive to other criminals. Changing and modifying behavior is a critical output.

The bottom line is that we need to strive to eliminate denial. We need to move forward on the basis of accepting the realities around us. We need to take into consideration existing threats, where we live or travel, what we do, and the fact that things can change and that we can't always rely on external parties, such as the police or private security agencies, to protect us. They may be doing the very best they can, but they have limited resources and limited reach. Criminals have almost all of the advantages. Referring to Margaret Thatcher during the IRA era, the IRA stated that they only have to be lucky once; she has to be lucky all the time. That's very true and translates directly to criminal activity and modus operandi (method of attack). To help understand this we talk about the C.O.I. triangle.

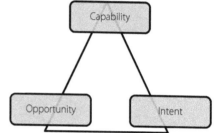

C – Capability of our opposition
O – Opportunity to commit the crime
I – Intent of our opposition

A triangle needs all three sides to stand and out of the C.O.I. the only variable that you can have some measure of control over is *opportunity*. As such we should focus on minimizing and removing the opportunity whilst we hope the authorities are focusing strategically on tacking the intent and capability.

If we look at some base principles and we focus on what we need to do in order not to become victims, we must now move to examining a few real core concepts. These core concepts become the building blocks to build a resilient and proactive habitual process that make you an unattractive and hard target to people seeking to harm you. It is also important at this point to understand what we refer to as the Whole of Person Model (WoPM). The WoPM refers to an integrative approach where we address three-dimensional reality of our lives which incorporates:

- Risk associated with our work lives
- Risk associated with our personal lives
- Risk involved with our virtual lives from a digital, cyber, and virtual presence perspective.

Let's briefly discuss technology.

Technology – a double edged sword

It's important for us to understand too, that in many cases as we've expanded technology and as technology has made our lives easier, where we can literally gain knowledge and information at any time, any place, or anywhere; so too can people with ill intent (Wolves). We've seen ongoing use of technology in the way terrorist attacks have been conducted; from the use of virtual chat rooms all the way through to live time geo-tracking and locational apps which have been applied during terrorist attacks globally. We also see the ongoing evolution of Cyber Crime and Hacking to the point that cyber threats are among the top corporate and governmental risk areas today.

> AS TECHNOLOGY HAS MADE OUR LIVES EASIER, THE SAME CAN BE SAID OF THOSE WITH ILL INTENT. KEEP IN MIND THAT THEY SHARE IN ALL THE ADVANTAGES THAT MODERN TECHNOLOGY OFFERS US AS LAW-ABIDING CITIZENS.

For us, it's important to understand that the new age of internet and global telecommunications and benefits of a linked world also come with a downside, where people can discover personal information about us and gain knowledge anytime they want. As such, you should be very careful as to what information you share and put on various other social media structures such as Facebook or Twitter. You should be careful around data and how you share and carry it as well as how you interact online on various websites and different types of communication platforms.

We should also be cognizant from a workplace perspective as to why there are so many cyber security initiatives put in place. As an example, if we look at spamming and phishing type email attacks, they continue to occur, which means there is some base of success for these attacks, even though it might be very small proportionately. The potential attacker is sitting wherever in the world they are, satisfied with a hit rate of one in ten million, so all they need do is just send out ten million emails via an automated process to get that one hit. While we may receive these emails and go *'well that's really silly', how could anybody click on that*, clearly people do, otherwise the attacks would not continue.

The core driver when it comes to technology is that we need to accept and understand that technology in many cases is a double-edged sword. It enables information, access, knowledge and data transfer for our potential attackers, just as it does for us as individuals trying to make our lives simpler and easier. We should also understand that nothing stays constant and your personal situation may change; where you work, what you do may change from time-to-time. As such your virtual and digital practices should also adapt as required.

Key concepts

The very first concept is closely aligned to what we have previously discussed – the concept of **eliminating denial and accepting reality**. If that base principle is not put in place, everything else contained in this book will not be of relevance. Simply because as you read these pages, you won't believe that it could ever happen to you and therefore won't receive the full benefit of the contents. Once you accept that unfortunately bad things can happen to good people, including you, we

> IT IS IMPORTANT THAT WE FOCUS MOST OF OUR EFFORTS ON PREVENTION AND AVOIDANCE.

can look to the concept of empowering you to take the necessary steps to avoid it happening. Building from acceptance is the idea of **striving for proactivity**. You can't undo the negative impacts of some violent crimes and even from a base exposure perspective, by planning ahead and developing a proactive attitude whereby we don't wait for bad things to happen, we try and focus on ensuring that they don't, which is a core fundamental attribute. This should not be confused with paranoia. We should focus on real threats and issues and ensure we do not waste time and energy on perceived issues. It is important that we focus most of our efforts on prevention and avoidance.

A guideline breakdown might look something like this (this is obviously subject to the environment and threat, based on where you are and what you are doing at the time):

- 80% of energy and resources into prevention and avoidance
- 10% of energy and resources on ensuring we could effectively manage a situation if it occurred
- 10% of energy and resources on ensuring we can recover afterwards

As per the well known 'Pareto principle' which highlights that we usually get 80% return from 20% of our activities, we need to focus on the idea of proactivity. This sounds very simple but we tend to be reactive by nature and do not take action until we have no choice or something has already happened. We have found over the years in consulting to 100's of organizations and blue-chip companies that because of the denial based approach combined with ignorance and negligence, most people tend to allocate resources as follows:

- 10% of energy and resources into prevention and avoidance
- 50% of energy and resources on ensuring we could effectively manage a situation if it occurred
- 40% of energy and resources on ensuring we can recover afterwards

From an individual perspective, I suggest that you seriously think about how you allocate your own resources, including time, effort and money. Try to get the equation to become a representation of a proactive approach instead of a reactive approach. In fact, learning self-defense is a proactive investment. This concept is expressed beautifully by the late Imi Lichtenfeld (Sde-Or)[1] founder of Krav Maga who was famous for

---

[1] I had the privilege to meet and visit with Imi when I was teaching and training in Israel in 1996. Whilst he was bedridden at this point, he was most willing to chat and share his opinions and thoughts.

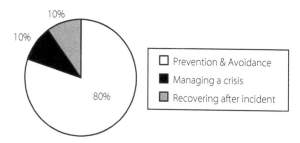

saying that people should learn self-defense "so that they may walk in peace". His dream was that every person, regardless of gender, race, nationality, age, fitness, size, or strength could learn to defend themselves and have a peaceful existence. In reality an integrated approach which covers Planning, Preparing, Responding and Recovering (PPRR) is very important regardless of what the balance is.

The next step we have to take is ***understanding reality***. We need to explore how attacks actually happen and why we respond the way we do. Our perceptions of both of these things are very often not in-sync with reality. Based on us learning about violence second hand or from television (we will discuss this in detail later in this chapter), we often perceive that we have a lot of time when attacked to think and work out what we would do. Unfortunately, nothing could be further from the truth.

In terms of how attacks happen, I have had some interesting experiences in my career. As part of our research into managing violent attack we've done 1000's of carjacking scenarios where we found that we could average out a carjacking in roughly 8 to 12 seconds. We even got to rob a bank. This was a bank in South Africa that had numerous security measures in place, including armed guards, access-controlled doors, a five-minute tactical response capability, bullet resistant screens protecting the tellers and various other early warning systems. We only had one opportunity to commit the robbery based on the expense and energy required to replace the bullet-resistant glass after breaking it. The reality is that it took us only around 1 minute 20 seconds to control the 20 to 30 people who volunteered to participate in the activity, get the cash and get out of the bank before the response capability was mobilized and able to respond.

In fact, when we look at personal attack, most people don't even realize they're in a fight or have been assaulted until they've already been struck or are on the ground. I can personally attest to this. In a few situations, and despite all of my training, I have either been struck first or been wrestling on the ground before I truly realized the attack was happening. Therefore, a critical component when it comes to being realistic is to understand that things will probably happen much quicker than we can actually imagine. This is especially true when we get an adrenal dump and become the recipient of all of the adrenal response signs and symptoms (this will be discussed later on in much depth). Therefore, the need for training and preparation is critical.

As with everything, there are always two sides. The other side of the coin, in terms of being realistic is, about our own abilities and response skills – in other words being honest about what we can and what we can't do when faced with violent or intense situations. Out of thousands of people we've trained, we've had experienced martial artists, we've had people who carry firearms in countries where they're able to do so and many others full of bravado and male ego. These people often say interesting things and have very unrealistic self-perceptions when participating in preventative training sessions. They state with much conviction things like *"but we could fight off an attacker or we would be able to shoot them before they could harm us"*. What's real and what's perceived are very important issues, and are sometimes worlds apart. Many things are possible but far fewer are probable. To clarify this, it is useful to understand what is sometimes called the law of diminishing options. This means that as we move closer to reality (i.e. more speed, more power and more consequence in an attack) there are far fewer things we can actually do. The law is explained in various ways but in essence highlights the following:

- At 30% speed and 30% power in a simulated attack almost anything is possible

- At 50% speed and 50% power in a simulated attack we lose ½ of the possible options
- At 80% speed and 80% power in a simulated attack roughly only 25% of what we think we can do is possible
- When dealing with a full speed, full power attack possibly only 5% of previous options are achievable, subject to the type of attack, the experience of the attacker and the defender and a few other related variables.

The dynamics of an attack is something we really have to take into account if we want to be realistic about what we can and can't do. A great example of this is what law enforcement officers refer to as the 21-foot or 7-meter rule. This rule basically highlights that at a range of 7 meters or more an officer would have the time necessary to be able to identify an attack, draw his firearm and successfully engage whilst creating what is referred to as safe separation from the target. At less than 7 meters, the officer would most likely not be able to draw his weapon and would land up getting stabbed or assaulted. In order to be effective and survive, the officer would therefore have to resolve the situation with an alternative type of tool, such as unarmed combat or self-defense first.

> THE CORE SECRET THAT ENABLES US TO MAXIMISE PERSONAL SAFETY IS MAKING PROACTIVE CHANGES IN OUR LIVES BASED ON REALITY…

In terms of translating and applying this concept we need to realistically admit that '*if I'm aware of my own personal space, ideally that should extend to 21 feet or 7 meters*', which in most cases in modern life is almost impossible. We therefore must once again make sure that our planning, our preparation, and our capabilities are tested, not just theoretical. Often people will tell us, '*if something happens, I'll just run away and when adrenalin kicks in, I'll be able to get away*'. Unfortunately, they disregard the fact that the attacker too has adrenalin raging through their body and is likely to be fitter and in better shape than most people who would be running away from that attack. The moral of the story is that if we want to empower ourselves to prevent becoming the victims of violence or minimize the chances of bad things happening to us and to be able to react correctly at a crucial hinge point, we have to plan ahead in a realistic fashion.

The next step is this idea of *integration*. While the hope is that most people would take the idea of personal safety very seriously, the reality is that most people do not allocate much time at all to this activity. In verbal feedback obtained from thousands of people we have trained, most people admit that they would possibly allocate at most an hour or two per week towards proactive personal safety activities. When digging deeper, we found that the average everyday person may honestly only be willing to allow for a few minutes a week, if that. If you analyze the field of personal safety in a more concrete manner and break it down into subfields, you would need to learn how to defend yourself; stay in shape; keep your first-aid up to date; ensure your driving skills were first class; and keep current with the basic threat assessments and scenario realities that are happening around you. This would roughly take you a minimum of four to six hours every week. When comparing the four-six hours with the few minutes most people are actually willing to allocate we see a huge discrepancy. In order to overcome this you therefore need to work on a little bit of cheat and try to maximize whatever time you are willing to allocate to personal safety as effectively as you can. The core secret that enables us to maximize the output based on the minimum time and effort investment is aligned to making habitual changes in what we do. Whilst this requires more work upfront and a healthy dose of self-discipline, it enables hard target outcomes to be achieved over time with the minimum amount of time and effort.

If we can just look to integrate some of the basics that we'll cover in the awareness section of this book, such as scanning the environment and the people there and teaching ourselves to identify exits and escape routes, over a period of time we could practice and apply these skills and make them habitual. These are the exact same skills that highly professional security personnel apply as second nature. It's not about being paranoid. It's simply about making sure that we have a plan and that we are aware of what's happening around us as opposed to walking around naively and thinking nothing bad will ever happen.

The idea of integrating these concepts into the way we live is nothing more than just admitting the realities of the world we live in today, based on some of the complex threats that we face. It might be something as simple as teaching yourself good, web-based and email behavior, where you ensure that you don't open emails from foreign sources or don't click on links that you haven't verified. If you don't make that a solid habit and you're not paying attention, chances are that before long your system may have been compromised and valuable data or information accessed.

Once we've grasped and integrated the first three principles of *acceptance, being realistic and integrating good habits into our daily practices* and they are firmly established, it's time to look at the next principle – ***flexibility and agility***. We need to continuously bear in mind the need for flexibility in our thoughts, patterns, and behavior. We also need to be agile enough to change course or adapt to quick changes when required. From an external threat perspective, the way criminals and terrorists select targets and commit attacks constantly changes. The modus operandi (method of attack), their focus and their targeting is constantly adapting. From an internal context, your own personal life and behaviors may change. You may change jobs; change where you live; you may get sick; you may get injured. All of these, would affect the likelihood of you being selected as the victim and your capability to respond. We should therefore ensure that we try to plan and prepare, based on principles, as opposed to trying to plan and prepare using fixed methods of doing things and being inflexible.

I would like to use an example from my own life to illustrate flexible thinking and adaptive behavior. As a young and single man, I was willing to expose myself to much more intense risks than I would do now. I was willing to go almost anywhere and do almost anything, but all of that has significantly changed now that I'm a husband and a father. The fact that my willingness to expose myself to risk might have a significant impact on my family means that I now seriously analyze the security and safety related aspects of job offers nationally and internationally before I make a decision. The core concept of flexibility is trying to be adaptable as required instead of trying to force your perceived realities into environments that are constantly changing. *Flexibility, agility* **and** *adaptability* are critical outputs if we're going to thrive in a fast-paced environment.

Resilience **and** *survivability* are the next foundational principles we need to assess. The ability to overcome hardship and carry on regardless of what life may throw at you is a critical skill and attribute required to thrive, especially if something traumatic or bad happens to you. One of my mentors – the late Major David M Sharp (Ret), was held as a prisoner of war during the Korean war. For almost 3 years, he had been subjected to ongoing torture and hardship, including being locked in a small box in solitary confinement for over a year. Whilst David had been a career soldier, some of the lessons he willingly shared have direct relevance for all of us. Firstly, he highlighted that **we should strive to not waste effort and emotions on things that we cannot influence and rather focus on our internal locus of control which we do have power over**. Secondly, he described how, when he had been a prisoner, he kept **a strong mental attitude with constant positive reinforcement** and kept reminding himself that no matter how bad things were for him, there were people elsewhere that had it worse. Now, being starved, beaten and locked in a small box is a pretty harsh situation but this approach worked for David who later went on to fulfill a long military and civilian career as an educator and consultant – it can work for you too in situations way less intense. You just need to remember that when things get tough, that is when the most strength (internal or external) is required. All of my martial arts students will quote me as highlighting to them during a particularly hard training session that **what counts is how we perform when we are tired, stressed and not at our best**. Anyone can perform well when everything is in their favor, but typically this is not when wolves will attack. Paranoia is very negative and should be eliminated – Walking around in a state of perpetual panic is will have an extremely negative effect on you and your life, but having a deep seated self confidence that you can perform in hard situations is a great level of comfort.

The final foundational principal is the concept of *logic*. If what I've explained in this book does not make sense to you, please contact us and share your concerns because as previously stated, you are the person who will have to apply it and this book is meant to be able to help you to do so more effectively. In all likelihood, if something doesn't make logical sense to you, you're less likely to accept it and therefore less likely to apply it, which means that the time and effort you are spending in gaining this knowledge may actually be wasted.

Key concepts in summary

One of the things we need to do is ensure we have a solid understanding of the base principles before we can look at actually applying core concepts and techniques that would help us stay safe. These core concepts are based on the need to accept that bad things may happen to us or people we care about. The need to accept that we may have to make minor changes to our lifestyles, adapt and make ourselves a hard or unattractive target through striving to eliminate denial is real. We need to make sure that we educate ourselves so that we are not ignorant and we should strive to ensure that we develop good habitual practice so that we're not negligent. We need to be realistic about our capabilities and about the way attacks actually happen. Developing an attitude of resilience and survivability based on integrating good habits into your daily lifestyle, while maintaining an attitude of flexibility and adaptability, is critical to success. Having a logical framework and foundation well in place to ensure that acceptance is possible at both a conscious and subconscious level is just as important. These aspects form the base building blocks for us to develop a fundamental personal safety and resilience behavioral pattern that would make you and your loved ones' unattractive targets to people with ill intent.

When we start trying to develop strategies, tactics, techniques and

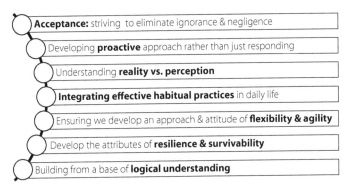

Acceptance: striving to eliminate ignorance & negligence

Developing **proactive** approach rather than just responding

Understanding **reality vs. perception**

Integrating effective habitual practices in daily life

Ensuring we develop an approach & attitude of **flexibility & agility**

Develop the attributes of **resilience & survivability**

Building from a base of **logical understanding**

approaches to enhance our own personal safety, we need to also remember that security and safety itself must be viewed as a compromise. Think about it – the most secure you could be would be to lock yourself in a high-security jail or no-access bank vault. In that case the quality of life that you would enjoy would be very, very low. Conversely, the least secure scenario could be you wondering the streets in a place you don't know inebriated or high on drugs. When looking at these two extreme options, whilst the examples may be far-fetched compared to the everyday person's normal lifestyle, the message is that security is about compromise. It's about finding how to enjoy the maximum quality of life. It's about being able to perform the maximum amount of activities that you want to enjoy, while adopting the correct security and safety measures appropriate to the threat and risk. It's much like balancing scales to make sure that they equal out based on what is required for each situation.

The core principles previously discussed in this chapter are the principles that help define what is required for you to plan and coordinate what you should be doing and what you may want to be doing so that we achieve realistic outputs. Many times, people have given me an example around wanting to behave a certain way because they feel that it is their God-given or human right to behave so. While this may be true, if that behavior exposes you to unnecessary vulnerability, then obviously it's not the smartest thing to do...

Risk approaches

One of the things we have to strive to achieve is to think things through in advance. Unfortunately, research has shown that human beings are not very good at fundamental risk management, otherwise we wouldn't be smoking, drinking or taking really unnecessary risks. The challenge is to find that balance, the DRE. If you want to partake in risky activities, how do you mitigate that risk to a degree that it's unlikely to have very serious consequences? This thought process has led to us developing what we refer to as the field of hard risk management. Hard risk management refers to an integrated approach to the way you manage your security, safety and all other related concepts; such as dealing with emergencies or being able to continue with your everyday life or your business operations despite interruptions such as natural disaster or other unforeseen circumstances. The basics of risk management refer to the ability to determine the likelihood and consequence attached to a specific issue or threat. In fact, the term risk is defined as the ***effect of uncertainty on objectives***.[2]

---

[2]See *ISO: 3100:2009 Risk Management Guidelines* for more information and guidance on risk terminology.

The core concept of managing hard risk is based on accepting that we can be empowered, but we need to integrate our solutions into a practical approach. Often people query and talk about the differences between safety and security or emergency response, but at the end of the day these should all be integrated functions. *Imagine a scenario where somebody knocks on your front door late at night. You go and have a look and you see that it's three large and aggressive drunk men. They're trying to kick your door down. Most people would agree that they'd call the police and would then implement various plans. They may try and get out of their house. They may try and find shelter inside the house, maybe in one of the rooms that is slightly more secure than the others... Worst case, they may try and find some sort of weapon in order to defend themselves in the event that the police don't arrive in time and these potential attackers break the door down.*

This methodology is often referred to as the run, hide, or fight approach. It aligns to our basic flight or fight instincts in terms of the way we would respond to a potentially violent attack. In reality, the idea of safety, i.e. the minimization of harm, the idea of security, i.e. all the major steps, techniques, approaches, methodologies and tools we would apply to create safety, and the idea of emergency response, i.e. the ability to apply relevant safety, security and/or rescue skills under intense stress, are totally aligned and are the basis of an interrelated approach. This approach is often referred to as the (DDDRR) detect, deter, delay, respond and recover approach or sometimes the defense-in-depth approach. The 'defense-in-depth' approach

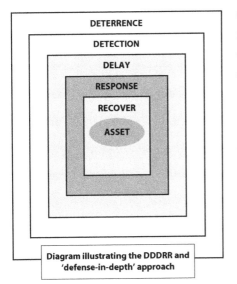

Diagram illustrating the DDDRR and 'defense-in-depth' approach

is that it's not just one activity that we do that would make us a hard target, but the process of many small activities we do that form layers around us and make us unattractive or hard targets to a potential attacker or would minimize the likelihood of somebody targeting your assets whether physical or web-based.

Humans are notoriously bad at assessing and focusing on risk realities. In fact, studies such as one from the United Kingdom National Health Service highlights how the leading causes of death are illness and disease, many of which are caused by bad diets, drinking, smoking and lack of exercise. The summary of the leading causes of death in the UK are illustrated in the diagram on the following page:

Leading causes of death in the UK[3]

Most of us go about our everyday lives continuing with these bad habits but being absolutely paranoid about issues such as crime or terrorism which, **in reality, when compared to our health, most other threats, risk and hazards, have a far lower chance of actually killing us**. Other risk issues such as being attacked by a shark become issues of dramatic concern when we think of swimming in the ocean whereas in reality, we are far more likely to get struck by lightning, hit by a car or even killed by a falling coconut when we look at statistical causes of death. When it comes to assessing risk, our goal should be to put it in perspective.

When we talk about perspective, the core point to understand is a base level of awareness (this will be discussed in depth in the next chapter) from a contextual overview in terms of which threats and hazards may actually harm us. Once we have established a base level, we can then zone in on a more tactical level, focusing on what's actually happening around

---

[3]NHS Atlas of Health. http://www.nhs.uk. Accessed 10 August 2015.

Leading Causes of Death in Perspective

- War
- Pregnancy & birth
- Medical complications
- Murder
- Undetermined events
- Mental health disorders
- Transport accidents
- Suicide
- Musculoskeletal disorders
- Diabetes
- Non-transport accidents
- Infections
- Kidney disorders
- Digestive disorders
- Nervous system disorders

Heart & circulatory disorders

Cancer

Respiratory disorders

us at any given time. When we put these skills together, we should have a base level understanding of what is real and what is not, along with the tactical ability to understand what is happening around us. This should help us comprehend things better, including the reality that terrorism is unlikely to disappear anytime soon and neither will crime. With these realities understood, we should be able to program what is likely, possible or probable, so that we can actually understand how we should plan and prepare for what may happen, based on a real appraisal and not second hand anecdotal information or an after-thought.

As an example: We should be very careful around racial/religious and ethnic stereotyping. If you could go back and ask many counter-terrorism experts from the 1980s about the profile of a terrorist in their era, they would often give you a very similar answer–something along the lines of *'a male aged 18 to 25 years old, very often of Middle Eastern descent, poorly educated and often with a predefined routine and travel history which enabled them to attend a terrorist training camp.'* In the '80s these terrorist camps operated in locations such as Libya. Today, we've seen the advent of female suicide bombers, children being used as suicide bombers, lone

VIOLENCE CAN BE PREDICTABLE IF WE KNOW WHAT TO LOOK FOR. WE DO NOT LIKE TO LOOK FOR EARLY WARNING SIGNS AS IT INVOLVES THINKING THE WORST OF PEOPLE & OUTCOMES WHICH MAKES US UNCOMFORTABLE...

wolf extremist attackers, some as young as 14 years old, qualified doctors and professionals committing attacks or planning to. This shows us that previous profiles are no longer applicable based on today's threats. We should be very careful not to profile in a way that cause us to develop tunnel-vision in our thought process or in our capability to truly identify potential threats.

We should also understand that things change and adapt accordingly. Just because somebody fits into a certain racial, historical or gender based grouping does not necessarily mean that they are a bad person or a potential attacker. Having said that, one of the core frustrations that many security and personal safety experts highlight is the denial around predicting violent behavior. Gavin de Becker[4] in his book, 'The Gift of Fear' highlights, this and explains that violence is something that people sometimes believe is totally unpredictable whereas there are always pre-incident indicators (PINS), if we understand what to look for (PINS) and we minimize our own denial responses, we can very often predict, mitigate, manage and ideally prevent and avoid violent behavior.

The problem is in order to do this; we have to look at the very dark side of human nature. Inevitably good and moral people don't like to think that both ourselves and other people have a dark side or the capability to cause harm. We need to consider that other people have differing perceptions of reality. In most cases, from an individual's perspective, they believe they are doing right or can justify their own actions, even when they know they are doing wrong. To most people, it

---

[4]For more information see: de Becker, Gavin. The Gift of Fear, back cover, Dell, 1997.

seems extreme that somebody could justify blowing up a school bus full of children as a good idea and in accord with a moral code or a moral belief. The simple fact is, from the terrorist or that person's perspective (if they are mentally disturbed) they believe they are doing the right thing or are able to justify their actions in their own minds.

Based on some of the issues discussed in this chapter, the need to understand and apply risk management as a dynamic skill set rather than as a separate discipline is very important. Whenever we need to make a decision, we are inevitably applying risk management and principles. Our goal should be to apply the very best decision making so that we can actively take advantage of opportunities whilst simultaneously mitigating the potential threats and hazards associated with such opportunities. This capability is what we refer to as Risk Intelligence (RI). I define RI as:

> **RI is a living skill and applied attribute that enables better decision making to proactively embrace opportunity and manage negative outcomes.**

Chapter summary

One of the outcomes of the experience of having a family member killed in violent crime was that I realized it truly doesn't matter how professional, competent and capable I am, because at a time when my family needed me there to protect them, I wasn't able to be there. This was a life-changing moment for me and led to me changing my thought process in terms of what I wanted to do. It likely changed my course in terms of focusing me, not only on how far I could push myself and what I could achieve in terms of my own capabilities, but it also enabled me to focus on how I could empower others. Leading on from this concept in terms of empowering you, the reader, is this idea that when we learn, we need to ensure we have some base framework principles that glue and connect our thought processes with our reactions and our understanding. Otherwise all we have is a bunch of concepts that float around in our subconscious memory which may or may not be there when we need them. As you read through the pages of this book, bear in mind that it is up to you. Change, modify, adapt, adjust, and refocus any of the material in a format that makes sense to you because at the end of the day, you are the one who may have to use it to protect yourself and your loved ones.

The truth of the matter is, it doesn't really matter how effective, capable or competent trainers, instructors, law enforcement officers or any of the other great people who work to empower and protect us are, they probably won't be there when you need them, otherwise an attack or a situation may not have occurred at all. The true lesson is that we need to empower ourselves, because the only person who is guaranteed to be there when things go wrong is *you*. If what you're taught and what you learn does not make sense, you're unlikely to use it at a critical juncture. We should focus on real threats and issues and not get distracted by media noise or hearsay, and try to apply the base levels of skills over time to build habitual behavior. In order to change your level of preparedness, I ask you to apply a simple exercise (the 3PC-S which you will learn about in Chapter 3) which will involve only 15–20 seconds a day for a continuous period of 21 days. After this, some of the base skills should become integrated into your everyday functioning. This habitual behavior is one of the greatest gifts you can give yourself should something truly bad happen.

Our goal as law abiding moral people should be to try and mitigate and minimize violent, criminal and negative behavior at its root wherever possible. However, in this modern day and age, we rarely are in an actual position to tackle these issues at their core. Where violent-based behavior – whether it be criminal or terrorist motivated – is the norm, it is very difficult to counter and may take generations on a societal level to achieve. For people who are negatively predisposed and/or in societal groups which have ingrained violent or extremist ideology, the instant access to information and technology makes it much easier for such people with ill intent to gain access to the knowledge, skills and guidance needed to conduct attacks.

The bottom line when it comes to understanding how to be proactive is that we need to look at how we can empower ourselves to lead healthier, safer and less stressful lives whilst being cognizant of the realities of this modern era. By understanding key principles and developing a base level of awareness and being conscious of the realities of crime, terrorism, cyber-attack and various other threats and hazards, we can mitigate the likelihood of these things happening to us. We tend to not want to acknowledge everyday issues that may affect us or the potential for bad things to happen or, in some cases, we become so fixated on the negatives and function in a state of paranoia which is as bad as not being aware at all. The unfortunate message is that these challenges are only going to get more intense as we go forward over the next few decades. We need to empower ourselves to support the authorities and support initiatives that are striving to minimize the impact of such negative activities as well as enhance our own personal family and wider circle safety structures, so that we can truly make a difference in creating a safer and less exposed world.

CHAPTER 2

Violence and Attack – What You Need to Know

What's real and what's not

Now that we have looked into the fundamental concepts needed to create a platform for proactive risk, security and personal safety, we need to dig a bit deeper into two issues, namely **fear and violence**. We need to define these foundational concepts in a practical way and ensure that we are able to capitalize on the survival-based benefits that fear brings, without getting caught up in the negatives such as anxiety, stress and paranoia. Similarly, when it comes to violence, we need to ensure we can at least have a base of comparison and understanding so that if we are confronted with it, we can manage it effectively. It's critically important that when we assess what's real and what's not, we understand the way attacks actually happen. With the evolution or devolution (depends on your perspective) of terrorist threats turning into small-scale lone wolf type attacks, the increase in, for example, active shooter incidents, knife crime, workplace violence and personal attacks are an ever present reality and core concern. Dave Grossman, is a former West Point psychology professor, professor of military science, and Army Ranger, in his books 'On Killing' and 'On Combat'[1] explores the how, why and

---

[1] *Grossman, D., with Christensen, L., On Combat: The Psychology and Physiology of Deadly Conflict in War and in Peace, Warrior Science Group Publications, 2004. (Published in Chinese, Japanese and Italian; on the USMC Commandant's required reading*

the related issues around humans killing each other; how we can be conditioned to kill and the consequences around that extreme decision as well as the manner in which sheepdogs need to prepare and manage stress and mental health for successful performance and quality of life. I would urge all readers to explore some of his findings because if we can understand and come to terms with the darkest parts of human nature, then it is a lot easier to cope with the everyday realities, which may be of a much less severe nature. In addition, an understanding of the role of sheepdogs and how they perform can only be of benefit in terms of releasing and nurturing your own inner sheepdog.

In the modern era we live in, we tend to learn about violence, and are influenced dramatically, by what we see and hear in the media and on TV. The proliferation of social media has also increased our exposure, and in many cases, misplaced our understanding of threats, issues and associated risk exposure. We have found that whilst most of us know that the media often exhibits some or other bias, there is a perception that what we see on the news is an accurate portrayal of what's actually happening globally. The fact that we can switch on the TV, switch on any of our various devices and in live time, be updated about incidents that are happening anywhere in the world creates a misconceived reality when it comes to threats and risks. We are often led to believe that things that are far away may actually pose imminent and significant threats to us. This in essence is the media's objective in many cases – to bring you into the story and make you feel as though you are there. Whereas in reality, what's shown on TV may have very little impact on you even though it is being portrayed in a way that makes you think and feel otherwise. Our ongoing exposure to media (both social and formal) creates a perception that in many cases threats are actually closer to home than

---

list: Grossman, D., On Killing: The Psychological Cost of Learning to Kill in War and Society, Little, Brown and Co, 1995 (hardback), 1996 (paperback), 2009 (revised edition), over a quarter of a million sold as of 2012. Nominated for the Pulitzer Prize for non-fiction, 1995.

they may really be. This is a complex issue, as knowing what is going on is important from a contextual threat perspective. Without doubt the media is an amazing source of data. However, the limitation of this is that, all of this data and information is stored in your subconscious memory, and will have a significant impact on the way you perceive your personal safety and the risks that you actually may be exposed to. We have all experienced people who watch the news and then present as though they are experts on a specific subject that they may have only just been made aware of on TV. This is an illustration of how effective conscious and subconscious media programming can be.

The important aspect in terms of context, is to remember that the media's aim is to make you watch and listen. In fact, when it comes to social media, it is even to get you to engage. I have had the pleasure of working with many journalists and have been interviewed by the media on many occasions. This is usually a great experience but every now and then, you can tell that the interviewer is pushing you into a corner to try and get you to say something in support of their bias or stance on an

> YOU NEED TO CRITICALLY EVALUATE WHAT YOU SEE IN THE MEDIA (BOTH FORMAL AND SOCIAL) AS IT MAY CREATE THE WRONG THREAT PERCEPTION. YOU NEED TO UNDERSTAND THAT MOST OF WHAT YOU LEARN FROM TV AND MOVIES IS NOT AN ACCURATE PORTRAYAL OF THE WAY VIOLENCE HAPPENS.

issue. Whilst there are many ethical and reputable reporters, journalists, and media representatives out there, at the end of the day, if you don't watch, read or listen, they don't stay on air. The critical reality for them is sensationalism. It hinges on driving interests and points that may not actually represent views or perspectives that are directly related to what may impact you or your loved ones and they are often indifferent about the consequences of long term exposure to issues such as terror attacks or violence on you and your perception of safety.

In terms of violence, the media is one of the places where we have the most exposure to violence and violent behavior. We tend to believe that just because we've seen and been exposed to violence on TV and in movies, we have some understanding of the way violence actually happens. Unfortunately, this is almost never the case. Real-life violence is often lightyears removed from how Hollywood portrays it. As an example, I am sure you could easily recall a TV show or a movie where the hero gets shot, kicked, stabbed, and assaulted, yet he's able to carry on and defeat the opposition. On the other hand, the bad guys get hit with one punch and are knocked out cold. We also see different, often inaccurate, realities in terms of the way we are able to identify attacks actually happening compared to what we have seen in the movies and on TV. As an example, on TV there is plenty of time for the hero to think and evaluate options and we can even see this happening in slow motion sometimes. In reality, this is not the case…

The inevitable problem is, if we program ourselves in the way we're going to respond to violence based on what we've seen on TV and the movies – which are entertainment driven – we are probably programming ourselves with the wrong information and prepping ourselves for the wrong type of reactions. It's critically important that we understand that in real attacks, you have very little time to make a decision. In fact, some experts estimate that you only really have between 0.3 and 0.5 of a second to make up your mind once an attack happens as to what you're going to do. This sets the stage for the reality that reactions need to be instinctive and reflexive, otherwise you will respond with the base fight or flight instinct which may not always be appropriate or in your best interests. Even worse, you may freeze or panic at a critical point, which may have

> WE SHOULD CRITICALLY ANALYSE WHAT WE LEARN FROM TV AND MOVIES AND NOT SIMPLY ACCEPT WHAT WE SEE AS REAL OR REPRESENTATIVE OF ACTUAL THREATS AND ISSUES.

significant negative consequences. This is a topic in its own right and Adrenal Response Management (A.R.M) will be addressed later on in this book in more detail.

In terms of other aspects of violence, you should realize that in any violent interaction, the likelihood is you will probably be hurt or injured even if you're highly trained. If there are knives or edged weapons involved, you will most likely get cut. If there are firearms involved, it's quite likely that the firearm may land up going off even if you play the situation perfectly. There are numerous books written on such attack situations – I suggest Gershon Ben Keren's[2] books on Krav Maga as an excellent starting point.

Another place we learn about violence is from hearsay and what other people tell us. I have generally found, in a career spanning more than two decades, where I have worked with men and women who live every day intimately engaged with violence as a career choice, that those who are used to violence don't talk about it much. In my experience, this occurs for two main reasons. Firstly, they have become so acclimatized to it that they believe everyone understands the harsh realities as they do, so there is no need to talk about it. Secondly, and more commonly, is where they feel that everyday people would never understand and that it's not worth trying to explain as they won't get it or they take an active decision to shelter the people around them from harsh realities so that they don't have to know how ugly the world can get. Because the people who really understand violence don't usually talk about it, it means that the people who usually do, in my experience, are typically making up all the so-called fights and dangerous situations they have been in. In support of this, one of our internal psychological protective measures is something called memory distortion/disruption. Memory distortion/disruption is a built-in protective mechanism that enables

---

[2]Krav Maga: Real World Solutions to Real World Violence by Gershon Ben Keren & Krav Maga Tactical Survival: Personal Safety in Action by Gershon Ben Keren and Miki Assulin.

us to recall really traumatic events in a somewhat dissociative manner, so that we don't relive the entire trauma every time we are reminded of it. I have experienced this on numerous occasions, both as a martial artist and as a security professional. I remember participating in one of the first MMA events in Africa in the early 2000s, I was fighting with broken ribs which I had hurt two weeks before the fight and despite some good advice, I foolishly decided to still fight. Whilst I had worked myself up, all I remember was the bell going and then the fight was over about a minute or two later. When I watched the video of the fight later, I was truly surprised as I did not remember most of the fight happening at all. On another occasion, we were conducting a security operation which included securing a venue for a large corporate client. We landed up having to remove certain people for being drunk and disorderly. This seemed to go as well as it could have until one of them struck a colleague of mine. It got blurry after that but I certainly don't recall being in a 'fight'. However, in the aftermath, I was told by several onlookers that I had dealt with two attackers and taken one down and restrained the other until help arrived. I have many more stories like these but you get the picture – in short, war stories from people claiming to have been in violent situations usually do not create a great source of realistic information on the way violence happens.

Referring back to Gavin de Becker's concept of pre-incident indicators (PINS). In his work, he talks about how we have the ability to be able to identify and predict violence, yet so many people believe you can't do this or that it is impossible. They believe violence is random and there are no early warning signs or precursors. In my opinion, I wholeheartedly support Gavin's take on the subject – of course we can predict violent behavior, we just have not been taught how to do this, or we've made a decision, whether consciously or subconsciously, that we don't want to! The perception of us not being able to predict violence simply lends to the earlier concepts that we previously discussed – the concepts of being either ignorant or negligent with a heavy dose of denial thrown in for good measure.

I have also found that there's a moral perspective to the understanding and acceptance of violence. Inevitably most people want to look for the good (or at least ignore the bad) and don't really want to take time to focus on the potential ugly or threatening characteristics of human nature, either in themselves or in others. This links with the fact that we don't like to spend time thinking about things that may have a negative outcome, such as being hurt, attacked, assaulted, raped or even murdered. The reality is that living with that level of denial simply disempowers us. It also empowers our attackers and the wolves that wish to prey on us, who are then able to perpetrate acts of crime and violence on an ongoing and regular basis because we don't know what to look for and, even if we think we do, we usually could not be bothered or just don't want to look for it. Even when we have seen it, we tend to rather want to ignore it and hope that it won't happen to us or that someone else will say or do something. It amazes me how many violent situations are now being filmed by spectators who later post them online but do not bother to help the victim who is getting assaulted or hurt. I accept the reasoning of wanting to film an incident so that there is evidence of what occurred but what often happens is someone gets killed and the person filming could possibly have stopped the situation. How does filming the incident help the victim then? This may actually be a manifestation of what is known as the '**bystander effect, or bystander apathy**', which is a social psychological phenomenon that refers to cases in which individuals do not offer any means of help to a victim when other people are present. The probability of help is inversely related to the number of bystanders. In other words, the greater the number of bystanders, the less likely it is that any one of

> IN MOST CASES, VIOLENT BEHAVIOUR IS PREDICTABLE. WE NEED TO KNOW WHAT TO LOOK FOR, BE WILLING TO ACTUALLY LOOK AND MORE IMPORTANTLY NOT GET CAUGHT IN THE BYSTANDER EFFECT AND ACTUALY DO SOMETHING.

them will help. Several variables help to explain why the bystander effect occurs. These variables include: ambiguity, cohesiveness, and diffusion of responsibility.[3] The goal is that by understanding the Bystander effect the next time you feel the need not to act when you see something happening, you can hopefully override it and do the right thing.

As a starting point, if we make the logical assumption that you, the reader of this book, would only utilize violence in protection of yourself and others as per the constructs of the law, we can then look at the most difficult issue. **Having to decide when to and when not to fight, or when to and when not to resort to violence, are very difficult decisions to make**. The consequences of using violence may have significant impact on several parties – for yourself; the potential assailant who you'll be using violence on, and who is using it on you or others; bystanders around you and even your family. If you were successful in defending yourself, there may be possible criminal consequences and other negative outputs arising from such behavior. If you decide to intervene in the protection of someone else, you my land up getting hurt as a consequence or face criminal charges for your good Samaritan initiative.

Leading on from this, the core concept of you defending yourself or others should be something that you need to think about ahead of time. In reality, when being faced with an attack situation, and even in spite of all the early pre-warning indicators, you would probably only have parts of a second to decide what your response is going to be. During that time, coupled with intense adrenal dump, it is next to impossible to be able to think of all the variable outcomes and consequences of whatever your decision may be. Obviously, there are more clear legal parameters and moral guidelines regarding the use of force and violence, particularly when it comes to self-defense when there is time to

---

[3]http://www.definitions.net/definition/bystander+effect (accessed: 10 November 2016).

weigh up all the variables – something which is certainly not the case when you or someone else is being attacked.

As such, I urge you to take into account a few core considerations in evaluating when you would and would not fight. Think about it, if you are not around, if you're wounded or injured in a criminal or terrorist incident, who will be there to look after your family? What sort of quality of life will you endure? Obviously, failure to act, or incorrect action may, in extreme circumstances, lead to the ultimate negative result – death. These realities are things that we tend to ignore simply because they're not palatable to think about, but by coming to terms with the worst parts of violence, we're able to better manage, perform, predict and mitigate the likelihood of these things happening.

As an example of consequence and action, let's think of a worst-case scenario. Imagine you're lying in your bed asleep alone in your house. You wake up in the middle of the night and there's an attacker over you with a knife at your throat. Do you instantaneously know what your reaction would be or do you have to hesitate and try and convince yourself that if this happened, you could cope with it, that you would have time to figure out how to deal with it? Whatever your response may be – whether it's to try to mitigate and manage the negative consequences of such a situation by cooperating with the attacker and hope he doesn't hurt you or whether it be to fight back – it is totally a personal choice. **The hard lesson is if you never thought about what you would do ahead of time, who knows how you will react?** Whilst there are obviously 1000's of variables that may come into play, if you are not sure of what to do and what you can do, there is a clear skills and knowledge gap.

I urge those of you who are parents or cohabit with people who you love, to think of the same scenario – an attacker with a knife at your throat, but imagine the knife was being held at the throat of your child or a dear loved one. What would the consequences of your action or inaction be then? Would you be willing to resort to violence to protect your child or loved one and keep them safe? In most cases, we found people unanimously answer yes. They would hesitate in many cases to protect themselves and use violence in defense of themselves, but to protect a child or loved one, most people would do whatever it takes. The reality however, is that if you're not around to protect them, who will be? Going back to a bigger picture perspective – even though the loved one you thought of in the above scenario may not be there at the time (as per our first example where you are alone), if you make the wrong call or the wrong decision, you may not be around and then the impact to your loved ones is huge.

In terms of understanding, mitigating and managing violence, and without going into a criminological, psychological, and societal overview of why violence occurs and how it happens, we need to accept a few realities. These realities align to the fact that most people are law-abiding moral citizens of whichever country they live in. Regardless of what their fundamental religious belief may be, they generally strive to be healthy and productive contributors to society. How-

> WE NEED TO ACCEPT THAT NOT EVERYONE PLACES THE SAME VALUE ON THE LAW AND YOUR RIGHT TO SAFETY AND YOU SHOULD NOT BE BLINKERED INTO THINKING THAT ALL PEOPLE ADOPT OUR VIEW OF MORAL AND HUMAN RIGHTS.

ever, there is a small minority who may hold extremist views and who may be wired slightly differently and lean towards psychopathic or sociopathic tendencies – the wolves. They think and act differently, they may, for example, not feel the same level of respect for your well-being as others do.

I've been very fortunate to work in many different places. At the time of writing this book, I've managed to visit over 20 countries, where I've trained, taught, been trained or conducted business. I've observed many different things and many different cultures. Among those, in certain locations and in various places in Africa, I've come across the sad phenomenon of 'child soldiers' – young people, sometimes as young as

9–10 years old – conscripted into paramilitary or military type service in a warped sense of hierarchy where 'might makes right' dominate.

In cases like these, you have to ask yourself whether someone like that child soldier, who has limited education, and even less options other than to carry a weapon of some sort and be exposed to extreme levels of violence, has already killed someone? If they make it to their late teens or early twenties, you can almost be assured that they, without question, have on numerous occasions had to use lethal force and commit some pretty extreme atrocities, otherwise they would probably not be alive themselves. Somebody like this who was not educated, raised by morally questionable role-models, who was taught to espouse violence as a way of life, exposed to drug abuse and 'might-makes-right' thought processes, will not necessarily have the same moral and legalistic approaches that most people have.

Imagine you visit a country where you come across people such as this… They see you, a foreigner, walking down the road, wearing jewelry, well dressed, enjoying yourself – looking happy and fulfilled. Their thought process in all likelihood will not be – "I would like to go to school and then university, work really hard, get an education, make more of myself so that I can afford to do nice things and have nice possessions like the person I'm looking at." It would most likely be something more akin to "Those are nice possessions. I will take them. If this person resists, I will kill them." Quite literally, in many places around the world, the value of human life is significantly less than a piece of jewelry, a mobile phone or any other item of value. We need to come to terms with this reality. We also need to understand that as our culture goes through many changes on a globalization and connectivity perspective, we're consistently exposing ourselves and our young people

> PARENTS SHOULD TRY AND LIMIT THEIR CHILDREN'S EXPOSURE TO VIOLENT TV, MOVIES AND VIDEO GAMES AS RESEARCH HAS SHOWN THAT EXCESSIVE EXPOSURE HAS SIGNIFICANT NEGATIVE IMPACT.

to varying levels of violence, virtually at the push of a button. This brings forth the worrying evolution of violence much closer to home…

Dave Grossman has conducted extensive research into the media and violence, violent video games and toys and how they have influenced, and are continuing to influence our up-and-coming generations. Unfortunately, his findings confirm that this exposure links directly to a predisposition that leans towards violent behavior and a lack of respect for authority and authoritative figures, such as police officers. There is little doubt that future generations will have a very different take and appetite for violent behaviour. In fact, Grossman and DeGaetano state that there is *"incontrovertible evidence, much of it based on recent major scientific studies and empirical research, that movies, TV, and video games are not just conditioning children to be violent – and unaware of the consequences of that violence – but are teaching the very mechanics of killing"*.[4]

Whilst playing video games or watching violent movies on their own, certainly would not be a direct influencer on somebody who is of a sane state of mind with a solid family and support system, in terms of committing violence or breaking the law, however, somebody who was already predisposed to negative thoughts, felt alienated and misunderstood, now gains the capability and tools to better develop those sides of their nature.

Andres Breivik,[5] who landed up committing violent atrocities including killing many children on an island in Norway, claims that he practiced and sharpened his skills by playing first-person-shooter video games. When he actually committed his attack, he stated that he found it very similar and actually easier than what he had encountered in the

---

[4]Source: Grossman, D and DeGaetano, G. (1999). *Stop teaching our kids to kill.* Crown Publishers, New York.

[5]http://www.telegraph.co.uk/technology/video-games/9272774/MPs-call-for-violent-video-game-ban-after-Breivik-claims-that-he-trained-on-Call-of-Duty-Modern-Warfare.html (accessed: 12 June 2016).

video games because in the real world many people just stood and froze which made them easier to shoot as opposed to trying to run away.

We see the media, violent video games and other media and digital channels providing exposure to violence and promoting acceptance and access to information on how to conduct violence, criminal attacks or even terrorist attacks. This is readily available on the internet, including comprehensive details on how to conduct terrorist attacks... Another issue is the prevalence and popularity of Mixed Martial Arts or MMA. In my opinion, after being exposed to the world of MMA for many years, it tends to show many of the negative aspects of violent behavior without the numerous positive reinforcements that traditional martial arts or traditional sports, such as boxing, often espouse. In many traditional martial arts schools, you cannot really engage in violent or dangerous technical activities until you have passed through certain stages, where your morals, your levels of respect and even in some cases your honor, as it may be defined in various doctrines, are tested. For example, one of my mentors Dr Dennis Hanover the founder of Survival Jujitsu talks about the 6 respects (Respect for God, one's country, Parents, Educators, Friends and one's self).[6] The Japanese Martial arts focus on the term Budo (Martial Way) highlighting that training in Martial Arts is a way of life, and in fact it is said that Modern Budō has no external enemy, only the internal enemy, one's ego that must be fought.[7] These processes have previously formed a vetting or sifting system to stop people who may utilize such skills and knowledge to hurt people, from gaining access – unfortunately, this is no longer the case...

Today, you can go and learn dangerous and often lethal skills in almost any mixed martial arts school located in most big cities, with the minimum amount of vetting or integrity testing. The skills and techniques

---

[6]http://www.dennis-hisardut.org.il/dennis-survival-foundation/?lang=en (accessed 30: November 2016).

[7]*Craig, Darrell Max (2002). Mugai Ryu – The Classical Samurai Art of Drawing the Sword. Boston, Mass.: YMAA Publication Center. p. 2.*

taught are very dangerous and should not be made easily available to just anyone off the street without some sort of vetting process. If we compare the capabilities of criminals or terrorists, who can easily gain high levels of competency via training in mixed martials arts or via training and up-skilling themselves through online education or other tools, and we compare this to the amount of training that law enforcement officers or other agents who are tasked with protecting society undergo, we see our protectors have a significant disadvantage and an ever-widening skills gap.

In summary, we need to accept that for numerous reasons, people may resort to violence. However, we cannot complete this discussion without taking into account alcohol and substance abuse related issues. People who may be considered typical and law abiding from a behavioral perspective but who partake in the use of various dangerous drugs, methamphetamines or other banned substances may, in a normal, sane state of mind, not be predisposed to violent behavior, but in an altered state of mind due to substance abuse, may not be in control of their actions or have the ability to work out, in a rational and practical manner, the consequences of their conduct and behavior. As such, they may land up attacking, hurting or harming other people even though they would never do that when not intoxicated or in a normal state of mind.

> IT IS NOW EASIER THAN EVER BEFORE FOR PEOPLE WITH ILL INTENT TO LEARN THE SKILLS THEY NEED TO HARM OTHERS…

Summary of why violence is an ongoing issue

We should realize that if we truly want to be safe and secure and minimize the likelihood or potential of us being involved or exposed to a violent attack, we should prepare ourselves for this. We need to understand that violence doesn't happen the way Hollywood or even the news media often portrays it. Violence is ugly. People get cut, hit, stabbed and injured. Conversely, we are often programmed by the movies we watch, where a good guy can get shot numerous times and carry on, but the bad guy gets struck once and he's out of the game. People may be predisposed to violence for numerous reasons including:

- Upbringing and morality limitations
- Mental and psychological issues
- Exposure to violence as a way of life based on social groups and behavior
- The TV, Media and Video game desensitization exposure
- Exposure to Mixed Martial arts and violent combat schools with no vetting
- Drugs, alcohol, and related substances being abused

Violent attack dissected

In terms of attack, there are numerous ways of describing the way attack could happen. Geoff Thompson, who has written numerous books on violence often refers to two types of attacks namely, a blast attack and a confidence attack. An example of a blast attack could be –

- You're walking down the street minding your own business and all of the sudden get struck or tackled from nowhere.

Confidence attacks are more common. A confidence attack is where –

- Somebody would attempt to gain confidence to perhaps enter into a building or to gain close proximity to your personal space so that they're within easy range to be able to overwhelm or injure you.

Simply put if we look at the realities of blast or confidence attacks, the attacker has the advantage of selecting the location, the time and the manner in which they will attack you. The only advantage you would have is hopefully being able to predict where you want to be and when the attack will happen and hopefully remove yourself in time or respond before the attacker gains momentum – as per the COI triangle previously discussed. Unfortunately, the fact that action is faster than reaction means that generally speaking, if the attacker is able to get momentum and move first, the likelihood of them succeeding is very high.

Fundamentally, a base understanding of violence is important in moving forward with this journey of resilience building and preparedness. While it may be unpalatable, we should accept that people have different perspectives and views on violence to what we have. While from a societal point of view, striving to reduce violent behavior and develop a more harmonistic society is a noble goal to strive for, we are certainly a long way from that in our modern societies. As such, we should prepare ourselves for the worst-case scenarios so that, ideally, if we ever had to, we could defend ourselves. Once again as Imi Lichtenfeld said, this is important "*So that one may walk in peace*".

In terms of looking at the way violent attack occurs, there are a few points that can help us to understand. We refer to them as the "Five Concepts of Real World Violence". These are aspects that we have most commonly found in the way that effective combative martial arts or self-defense systems determine how people should defend themselves and are also consistent with the way that most attackers select and attack their victims. It's important for us, when we look at how we actually protect ourselves, to understand these core concepts. The *Five Concepts of Real World Violence* are the evaluation criteria that you can use to measure a defensive system in terms of whether it is preparing its proponents to deal with real violence or not. It can be represented as follows:

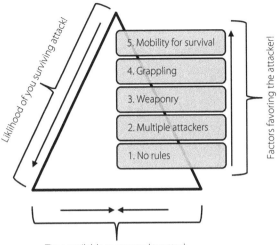

Time available to respond to attack

Before going into the details of the five concepts of real-world violence, let's examine the above figure briefly. The boxes 1–5 represent the tactical advantages the seasoned attackers will have over their target. The quicker the attackers get all 5 tactical advantages into play, the less time you, as the victim will have to respond, and the less likely it will be that you walk away from the attack unscathed! Conversely, if you have prepared yourself to the best of your ability for such a realistic attack, your chances for survival increases exponentially. The earlier you pick up the warning signs, the more likely you can avoid the attack altogether. A little bit later in this book we will have a look at how we can empower you to respond positively to such warning signs. Let's look at these five concepts in more detail now.

Concept # 1 – No rules

Number one concept is the reality of *NO RULES* – by definition, when people attack you, they disregard the law and they disregard your physical well-being and as such, their mindset and their mentality in essence is a mindset of no rules. Generally speaking, somebody who would attack another human would disregard the law because in almost all countries that espouse basic human rights – physical violence and the sanctity of your own body are usually accepted as base human rights. Somebody who would attack you would be clearly disregarding the law as well as any other moral binding considerations with regard to somebody else's physical well-being. If you planned to defend yourself using limitations, such as not being willing to stick your fingers in an attacker's eye, or you were not willing to strike them in the groin, or take a pencil and stab it into their face, you are at a significant disadvantage because your attacker is not bound by any of these limitations.

> THERE ARE ONLY TWO REASONS PEOPLE EVER FIGHT: **EGO OR SURVIVAL**.

There are only two reasons people ever fight – ego or survival. If it is an ego-based reason, the full might of the law may be the consequence of your action if you harm another human without the necessity to do so, but if it is truly a survival based reason, where you have no other choice but to defend yourself or someone else, then what do you have to lose? If you limit yourself to what you are willing to do, limit what you can and can't do, all you do is empower your attacker. Understanding this approach of 'no rules' helps you 'switch on' your own internal aggression and develop the capability to fight back if you need to.

When we learn self-defense, we often perceive how we will respond to a violent attack and we very often limit ourselves to what we believe may be fair, right, ethical or in line with the rules of some sort of combat system that we may have trained in, such as boxing or Judo. Even modern day MMA has rules designed to protect the fighters, such as no eye-gouging and no direct striking to the throat or the spine. These are all options that enable the smaller, weaker person to potentially beat a bigger, stronger person and if you are fighting for your life may be necessary options.

It is important to understand this reality – that there are only two reasons in life people ever resort to violence – survival or ego. Think about it carefully – no matter how hard you try, I guarantee you will be able to, in the end, divide any violent interaction into one of those two reasons. While it may seem a far stretch to put issues such as political or religious persuasion and moral righteous beliefs into the category of ego, the reality is that if a situation is avoidable, it would then not fall into the survival category simply because with control of ego, emotion and perception, you may be able to avoid that situation altogether or find non-violent recourse. We therefore have to understand that from your own internal matrix and understanding of behavior, if you're able to control yourself and program yourself to never respond based on ego-type stimulators or triggers, the only time you would ever have to resort to violence would then be for a survival based reason. If it's a survival-based reason, the core strategy is for you to get out of there and escape but if that is not possible, then fighting back may be your only option. This leads to the Run, Hide, Fight and Communicate Approach and Adrenal Response Management which will be discussed in detail later in this book but we will touch on it here.

Our primary course of action should always be to run and escape. Secondly, our goal would be to hide or shelter if we couldn't get away. Lastly, it would simply be to survive, which would involve fighting with everything you have or, in some extreme cases, cooperating with an attacker to ensure you stay alive long enough to hopefully get rescued or released, or at the very minimum, find a better opportunity to fight back than may be currently available.

> **IF YOU'RE FIGHTING FAIRLY IN A SURVIVAL SITUATION, YOU'RE DOING IT WRONG…**

In terms of knowing when to unleash your inner sheepdog and take on the role of protector, we should assess very clearly when something is an ego or survival based incident. The bottom line is, if it's a survival based incident and you can't run, hide or avoid it the concept of NO RULES is a crucial survival mentality. If you go into a survival based situation with the perception that there are rules and guidelines, you're always going to be on the back foot dealing with an attacker who is not bound by the same perceived limitations. Whilst this certainly does not mean that we disregard the law, however if your life is on the line what do you have to lose?

Concept # 2 – Multiple attackers

The next unfortunate reality of violence is that we very rarely get attacked by one person, from the front, when you are ready to defend yourself. As such the next core concept of real world violence is the principle of multiple attackers. In most martial arts or defensive systems, we generally learn to defend ourselves from one attacker, coming from the front, who only engages after a signal of readiness, such as a bell ringing or a referee sounding a buzzer. In reality, we get attacked from the sides and the back when we are unprepared, usually by more than one attacker. While it is a challenge to defend against just one, defending against two or three is achievable, albeit difficult. If you ignore this reality, your ability to respond is significantly compromised.

Most attackers will catch you when you're unaware and approach from the sides or back and be coming in groups, which means that when we plan and rehearse our reactions and we think about self-defense, we need to be practical about the way attacks will actually happen. You might spend a lot of time, effort and energy learning a self-defense system which only covers attacks from the front and delivered when you're

MOST ATTACKS OCCUR FROM THE SIDES OR BACK BY MULTIPLE ATTACKERS WHO ATTACK WHEN YOU ARE LEAST PREPARED.

ready to fight in a structured and rigid manner. This instantly programs you with the wrong reactionary stimulus because you're primed to look forward, wait for a ready cue and identify an attacker coming from the front only, whereas in reality you may get taken by surprise from the sides or back. The exception to the multiple attacker concept is usually sexual assault, whilst the attack still may come from the side or back.

It is often perpetrated by someone that the victim knows and is at least comfortable to be alone with or in close proximity to.

Concept # 3 – Weaponry

The next concept of real world violence we talk about is the concept of weaponry. Very few self-respecting criminals or terrorists will attack you unarmed. The use of weapons for most criminals or terrorists is a force enhancer and multiplier and helps them generate a better output from their perspective – i.e. more fear, more damage, etc. We therefore need to prepare ourselves for that reality. Now, I'm certainly not stating that everybody should become pro-gun activists and carry weaponry with them everywhere, but there is a logical thought process that says if we believe that in an extreme situation we may be confronted with weaponry, it's probably a good idea to at the very minimum, have a proactive base of understanding of how a potential weapon system may be used against you. This is important based on the small chance you may end up with that tool in your hands to defend

> IT'S HARD TO DEFEND AGAINST A WEAPON UNLESS WE HAVE A BASE KNOWLEDGE OF HOW IT WORKS…

yourself, your family or people who are around you. Very few criminals, if any, would attack you unarmed. Weapons are great tools that produce excellent results for the criminals utilizing them. As such, criminals will seek to arm themselves as effectively as possible. The truth of the matter is, if you do not know how a weapon works, the ability to defend against it is dramatically reduced. You don't have to be an expert in its machinations, but a base understanding could mean the difference between life and death. If you fear exposure, for example, to a firearm or a knife attack, it would make sense to at least have a fundamental understanding of how these tools may be used to harm you so that you know how the attacker may come at you and you also have a base idea of how, if you needed to fight with these tools, you could defend yourself.

As an adjunct to this, I have found from conducting training in environments where a lot of people do carry weapons, that they often don't realize the requirements for and responsibilities of carrying such weapons. In fact, the majority of people in my experience who carry firearms do not take the time to maintain the relevant combat readiness and handling skills and are often more of a liability because they have the weapon and think they can deploy it but actually can't when it counts. If you are person who carries a weapon, you should train with it often and in a realistic manner, otherwise leave it in the safe at home for worst case scenarios. This topic could form a chapter in its own right but the short message is that of responsible and capable ownership. Simply shooting at a two-dimensional static target once a year is not nearly enough to utilize a firearm in a combat situation and people should take responsibility to ensure that they develop and maintain the appropriate safe handling and usage skills that are required. This is applicable to all other self-protection tools too – such as pepper sprays or electronic control devices (ECD's) such as Tasers.

Understanding improvised weapons and defensive tools in your surroundings is also a critical output. The difference is that an attacker will utilize an improvised weapon against you where you may utilize an object in your environment as a defensive tool – simply because you don't attack people, as such you are always defending – even if its offensive defense, there are defensive tools around you that you could use to protect yourself, that may mean the difference between life and death. Conversely, if there are items in your surroundings that your attacker may be able to use against you as improvised weapons, you may land up being severely injured purely based on things that they could get hold of. **The bottom line with weaponry is if we don't know how a weapon works, fighting against it is an exceptionally difficult thing to do.**

Concept # 4 – Grappling and ground-fighting reality

The next concept of real world violence we refer to as 'the grappling and ground fighting reality.' We've seen this concept demonstrated through the evolution of mixed martial arts which shows us that the majority of fight situations, unfortunately, land up at close range and very often land up going to the ground. This is simply a reality we must accept and become comfortable with. We need to program ourselves that we could land up on the ground and should have some base way of maneuvering for an effective position, damaging the attacker and getting to our feet so that we can run away. The concept of grappling from a self-defense or personal safety perspective relates to the reality that a large amount of violent interactions end-up taking place at an exceptionally close range and in many cases, in fact the majority of cases, end up on the ground. This happens for numerous reasons, including issues such as the fact that when we're attacked we're usually not attacked in a wide-open space, and there are often obstacles around us that could cause us to trip or fall down. Inevitably, because of adrenal distortion factors, including loss of spatial perspective, we very often are so disorientated that we grab hold of the attacker whereupon the attacker very often grabs us (or vice versa) back and we both go down to the ground. In addition, because of tactical disorientation, when we're not too sure from where the attacks are coming from exactly, or what is happening, very often we actually land up tripping or falling as we try to run away in order to escape a potential attack situation. The truth is that whilst we are not suggesting that you should become a world champion ground fighter – which would be amazing if you had the time, effort and energy – you should, at the very least, consider how to perform should you find yourself on the ground, grappling for position and advantage so you can get back to your feet and escape. Keep in mind that the longer you're on the ground, the more damage may be inflicted upon you by multiple attackers who are armed and who are not fighting according to any rules…

Concept # 5 – Mobility is vital to survival

Our final concept of real world violence is what we refer to as the concept of mobility. The concept of mobility is also critical to understanding basic self-protection. If I am on the ground, I can't run, I can't escape, I can't find defensive tools in my environment to defend myself with, which makes me a much easier target to overcome. Ground fighting is also a tough skill to develop and takes a long time. Therefore, we should strive not to land up on the ground and try and stay on our feet so we can escape wherever possible.

Most fights unfortunately go to the ground for the following reasons –

- because there are usually multiple attackers;
- because they're likely to be armed;
- because there are no rules;
- and because you are very often taken by surprise when you're attacked, we need to really try and ensure that the core concept of trying to avoid an attack is our first priority.

However, if it is unavoidable and you have to fight, then the goal should be to **intercept** the attack, to **control** the attack situation and as soon as possible **escape** when safe to do so. We refer to this as the I.C.E. principle. If our goal is truly to escape, we should really be looking at how to stay mobile and stay on our feet, as you can't run away when you are on the ground.

IF YOU HAVE TO FIGHT AND HAVE NO CHOICE REMEMBER THE **I.C.E** PRINCIPLE:
- TRY AND **I**NTERCEPT THE ATTACK
- TRY AND **C**ONTROL THE ATTACK SITUATION
- **E**SCAPE AS SOON AS IT IS SAFE TO DO SO

If you go down on the ground, the surface itself may hurt you too. In addition, multiple attackers will have a much better chance of injuring you or controlling you. It will also be very difficult for you to run away and escape, or access improvised defensive tools in the environment to defend yourself with. **Therefore, as a primary goal of realistic self-protection and self-defense, we should be to stay on our feet as opposed to going down on the ground**, which may cause significant problems if it happens.

Summary of the 5 concepts of real world violence

In summary, these five concepts of real world violence, namely:

* no rules;
* multiple attackers;
* weaponry;
* grappling and ground fighting;
* and the primary need for mobility.

are critical success factors for you to prepare for and understand the way that attacks usually occur. Our core objective is to prevent and avoid a situation thus hopefully ensuring that you never have to use violence to defend yourself, but if you do, at the very least you will have a non-blinkered approach to these realities. You should understand that you can survive but will probably get hit, get hurt, and if there are knives, you may get stabbed, and if there are firearms, you may get shot purposely or by mistake if a shot goes off. However, we should not underestimate how tough and resilient the human body is, especially when driven by a focused and trained mindset. By understanding, that if you don't defend yourself and you are absolutely sure that the situation is a survival based situation and that you may die or get critically injured regardless of whether you cooperate or not, makes it easier to plan for when and when not to fight.

Several years ago we had a lady by the name of Cathy[8] – who came to a one-day women's self-defense course. While she seemed to want to be there, she was really not the ideal candidate for such a course. In fact, Cathy had poor coordination and just did not seem to 'get it'. However, she worked hard through the day and was able to manifest enough aggression to fight when she had to during the scenario phase at the end of the program. The course ended and we thought nothing further about her until about a week later, when we got a telephone call from her. Cathy sounded really strange, but she proceeded to tell us that she had been attacked the day before by two men who she was sure were going to rape her and then kill her. She remembered the lessons she had been taught and managed to fight them both off and escape. They broke her jaw (that's why she was talking funny) and she broke her hand striking them but she was thrilled and totally relieved that she was still with us. There are many more success stories like Cathy's but the lesson learned here is that a little bit of knowledge and preparation may be the critical success factor when your life depends on it.

Chapter summary

To reiterate and summarize the core concepts that we should put in place in order to create a base platform for understanding and managing violence, we need to keep the following in mind:

- Be realistic about the way attacks happen.
- When the media educates us on violence and when we watch TV and see incidents happening all over the world, we should use them as learning tools and see and understand these things in context.

---

[8]This is not her real name as she previously requested we don't share it but could use her story as an example.

- The reality is that at any given time there are millions of incidents occurring all over the world. Does that have a direct reflection on you? Well, that depends on your own personal surroundings, your own personal circumstance and your ability to conduct your own personal safety assessments which we will talk about in later chapters.

- It is critically important that we evaluate what is threatening to us and what is not so we can prepare for real threats and do not get distracted and waste effort and energy on things that may have no relevance or impact based on your personal situation.

- The other side of media exposure to violence hinges on the fact that continuous exposure to it may be having significant negative effects on us and our children. There is little doubt that future generations will have a very different take and appetite for violent behavior.

We should understand the core concepts around the way violence actually happens as opposed to the way we perceive violence happening, so that we can ensure that we program our responses effectively. We need to understand that unfortunately, even if we behave in the most effective way possible, sometimes bad things do just happen to good people. Based on training thousands of people and analyzing thousands of case examples, we estimate that roughly 90% of all situations are probably avoidable. Then there is that 5% which we group into the 'wrong place, wrong time or unlucky category'. Finally, the last 5% are attacks or situations perpetrated by highly trained professionals that may be very hard to avoid and/or prevent or where no matter who you are or what you've done, you may be targeted. But if we look at the potential to mitigate, avoid or minimize exposure in 90% of situations that could arise, those are pretty good odds. By understanding the 5 concepts of real world violence and preparing ourselves, we can minimize the likelihood of ever being exposed to violence if we have to improve our chances of survival if we have no choice but to fight.

CHAPTER 3

Applied Awareness

Focusing on prevention as the primary aim

Hopefully, whilst the likelihood of you ever having to use or apply defensive strategies and directly having to counter violent attack is very low, unfortunately sometimes bad things do happen to good people. If you want to achieve maximum enjoyment of the world we live in, such as travel or simply being able to move around in your everyday life without the impinging fear and concern of what to do if something truly went wrong; if you'd like to understand and feel that you have the confidence to properly assess what is safe and what is not, and to effectively determine how and when you should be able to conduct activities to minimize the chance of something going wrong, then this section is of critical importance for you.

Any preventative approach or any incident minimization strategy starts with a base understanding of what may happen and how likely it is to occur. Only then can we assess what our response may need to be, should something negative actually occur. In terms of simplified risk management, we often refer to this shorthand risk approach or risk process as the idea of establishing context, determining likelihood and consequence, and then determining how to implement measures that would reduce the consequence and/or likelihood to acceptable levels. None of this can be achieved without an effective understanding of context, i.e. what's normal and what is not. From an awareness perspective, we will talk about this concept as *base lining*. **The core idea of base lining is**

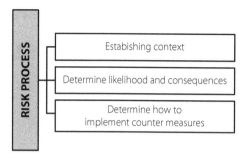

quite simply that if you do not have the basic context of what fits into your environment and if you do not understand what is normal or what is not, then it will be very difficult to determine what is suspicious or out of the ordinary. The focus here is being able to determine what is suspicious or out of the ordinary in the environment around you as well as in terms of the way people in the environment are behaving. If you are unable to do this, then it's very difficult to focus on predicting, avoiding and, worst-case, managing potentially dangerous situations.

Over many years, we've trained thousands of different people from different cultural backgrounds in the concepts of awareness and observation. These are practical skills that are very important and form the basis for what is referred to as situational awareness. The core premise is to understand what we are really looking for and then to learn how to make awareness an integrated and natural process so that it happens without paranoia, panic or fear. Once this is achieved, you are able to go about your everyday life knowing that you've primed your senses and honed your subconscious to focus on the issues that may cause you harm. Intuitively, you should be able to identify and measure things that are real, versus those that are perceived. In other words, what the aspects are that may actually cause you harm versus, what you think may cause you harm.

Ask yourself honestly – how often, if ever, do you sit around and actually discuss what really is dangerous and what really could cause you harm in your daily life? As previously discussed – humans are not very good at risk management in this fast paced and dynamic modern world. In fact, if we understood real risk management to a greater degree, there's a very high likelihood we would see nobody smoking, healthier

> THE BASE LINE OF AWARENESS IS THAT CRITICAL UNDERSTATING OF HOW I NEED TO ACT, BEHAVE, SCAN MY ENVIRONMENT AND BE ABLE TO TRULY MEASURE WHAT MAY GO WRONG FROM A PLATFORM OF REAL THREAT AS OPPOSED TO INACCURATE PERCEPTIONS.

eating and more people exercising appropriately. Instead we see people justifying risky behavior in terms of being negligent, ignorant and embodying a heavy dose of denial or just being too lazy to change bad habits or negative routines. **The truth is the core risks we face are often health-driven risks and as such our awareness of our own health and body are critical aspects for wellbeing.** While we may sometimes be paranoid because of media exposure to crime and violence, along with the thought of being in the wrong place at the wrong time when a terrorist attack which may strike fear into you, we should really and truly look at our awareness or levels of acceptance as a holistic approach in terms of how we could lead a healthier, safer and less-stressed life.

Our belief is that in terms of crime, violence and exposure to terrorism or fraudulent activities, roughly 90% of all activities are avoidable, but in order to avoid them you have to do some work. The difficulty is that most people are not willing to do this work in order to be able to predict what may go wrong and in thinking of worst case scenarios and planning, training and programming their reactions accordingly. We often tend to think that this is the sole realm of the authorities – that it's the responsibility of the sheep-dogs who get paid to deal with these issues. Fortunately, in most first world countries, governments have very capable agencies doing their best to keep their citizens safe. However, as discussed in earlier chapters, changes in technology, changes in globalization, new radicalized approaches to terrorist attacks from a lone wolf, low-level type attack methodology could pose significant threats and dangers. Wouldn't you want to just have the confidence to know that you are able to protect yourself and your family and that the basic activities and the way you conduct yourself instinctively every day, are, in themselves, deterrents, making you a harder and less attractive target and making your entire community safer?

I am sure you agree with this goal. The base line of awareness is that critical understating of how I need to act, behave, scan my environment and be able to truly measure what may go wrong from a platform of real threat as opposed to inaccurate perceptions. Once we're able to achieve that level of habitual behavior and focus on what truly may cause us harm or what truly is suspicious or out of the ordinary, as opposed to what we perceive, we're better able to deal with it. This needs to focus on two levels:

1. *Internal awareness and understanding of self – if you do not know your own state of mind and physical capabilities at any given time it is very hard to align real awareness with the environment. We are dramatically impacted by how we think and feel. Things that you may just brush off as non-issues when you feel physically well and are in a good mood could become major issues when you are not. A great example of this is road rage. When you are in a good mood and someone cuts you off the impact is far less than when you are already irritable.*

2. *External awareness – the awareness of your environment and the people in it as well the application of your ability to apply your senses to gather information of these aspects.*

Without an ability to apply both aspects (internal and external awareness) it is almost impossible to gain accurate context and apply effective awareness practices. When we are able to understand and apply both aspects, we can often rest easier knowing that intuitively we are assessing threats, risks and opportunities effectively.

Intuition – the starting point of proactive awareness

The starting point of awareness is an understanding of intuition. Over the years, I've asked thousands of people who we've trained to describe intuition. Amazingly, everybody knows what it is, everybody understands its core concept, yet, they struggle to actually quantify and explain intuition in a practical way. Whilst the work of people such as Gavin de Becker, Geoff Thompson and numerous others go a long way in helping define the concept and principles, we found that a systemized approach is critical for people to understand, accept and utilize their natural intuitive abilities. While we have to make some base assumptions, to communicate this methodology effectively, these assumptions are all aligned to scientific thought and to proven success from having trained thousands of people how to utilize their natural capabilities effectively.

When people discuss intuition, we often hear sayings like 'if there is doubt, there is no doubt', or "if in doubt, check it out." We are encouraged to have innate trust in our gut instincts even though many people resist this. If you get that intuitive feeling that something is wrong, if you get some of the following signs and symptoms which may include; butterflies in the stomach, hairs on the back of your neck standing up, cold shivers, heart rate beating faster, or just a sense of ill at ease, you know your intuition is telling you something. All of these are signs of your early warning fight or flight instincts kicking in. Your body is preparing to respond to some sort of danger or threat (real or perceived) that you have not yet consciously identified but has triggered a subconscious response.

To really understand intuition, we need to look at a few variables. The first concept is that everything we see, hear, taste, touch and experience is stored in our subconscious memory. This is a very important fact. As an example, if you've ever written an exam and have sat there and struggled to recall the correct answer, even though you know that you know what it is, you know how hard it sometimes is to create a solid link between conscious and subconscious memory. The way it works is that our mind acts like a supercomputer – everything we see, hear, taste, touch, experience or are exposed to, is stored in our subconscious memory – we have a massive pool of data readily available. Unfortunately, it's not always easy to readily access this information at will. Another consideration is that as with any system the output of the data is only as good as the data that is stored…

As an example of the capability of our subconscious mind, consciously, it's estimated that if I walk down the street and focus on what's happening around me, I could analyze roughly 8 to 10 pieces or bits of information a second. Subconsciously, I'm likely to be absorbing between 2000 and 3000 pieces of information. Is it hot? Is it cold? What does the ground feel like on my feet? Is the wind blowing? What do I smell? What's happening further away? What do I hear? These are all things that your subconscious is busy absorbing and analyzing while consciously we may have no thought process around these issues whatsoever. Only when our mind comes across something of interest to us or something that may be threatening do we get notified. As such our perception of the world is really based on what we are able to filter at any given time. In his book, Thinking Fast and Slow,[1] Nobel Prize winning psychologist Daniel Kahneman describes two types of systems that our brains apply to cope with all of this data. According to Kahneman, we can think about our brains as having two systems – super fast, automatic, intuition-based 'system 1' (S1) and effortful, reasoning-based, and much slower 'system 2' (S2). Most of our daily decisions are produced by S1, are automatic and are based on habits. They require little attention or effort. Through experience S1 allows us to become experts who can make fast, intuitive and mostly good decisions.

All we have to do is look at the way someone gets distracted when walking and talking on a mobile phone or listening to music, to see how incapable humans often are at multitasking and how easily distracted we get when the conscious is focused on a specific activity. When you get that

_____

[1] For more information see Kahneman, D. (2011) *Thinking, Fast and Slow*, Farrar, Straus and Giroux, ISBN 978-0374275631.

intuitive feeling – in reality, it is quite likely you might have seen, heard, smelt or noticed something out of the ordinary, which relates to information stored at the subconscious memory level. These links are made at lightning speed. You may not even have time to consciously piece together why you feel this intuitive feeling which is telling you that something is wrong or something bad is about to happen. The truth is your intuitive response is referencing data previously loaded into your subconscious memory, correlating it with input and information absorbed from your immediate surroundings, and processing a response faster than your conscious mind can keep up with. Later on when you have time to think about this, you may or may not be able to work out how and why this happened.

There are many research-based case examples where victims of crime have admitted to having a really strong intuitive feeling that something was wrong before something bad happened to them. In many cases, victims stated that they didn't act on that early warning and that this was the primary reason that they became a victim of crime. Reasons for not trusting our intuitive responses are far ranging. In discussing this with thousands of people over the years – there are many reasons given. The most common reasons people give for ignoring their intuition is they did not want to be rude and offend somebody who they think may or may not want cause them harm, or simply they were lazy and did not want to be inconvenienced, or simply thought that they were just being paranoid, after all why would anyone want to hurt them…

As an example, *If you imagine yourself walking home one night and there's a short cut through a park, you look into the park and everything looks okay, but for some reason your gut instinct starts to tingle and you think that this shortcut may not be the best idea. The downside of you trusting your intuition is the inconvenience of having to walk further instead of taking the shortcut through the park, but what happens if that inconvenience could mean that your life is saved and that you're far less likely to become a victim of serious crime?* I am sure you agree that this minor inconvenience doesn't seem like a big price to pay. *What happens if you were a woman alone and you had a bad feeling about some strange man following you into a building or walking down the street after you, following you towards your house?* Imagine as your intuition kicked in, if you went to a safe haven, never went home or found a place with other people – this may be an inconvenience to you, but it may be enough to stop a would-be attacker or rapist!

The reality is very simple. It is impossible for me, as the author of this book, to actually sit with you and work through all of your fears and preconceived ideas. This is where base understanding of fear is really important. Geoff Thompson in his book *Fear: The Friend of Exceptional People – Techniques in Controlling Fear,*[2] discusses two different types of fear. He highlights the difference between real fear and perceived fear. Real fear heightens our survival instincts and causes us to function at a higher output in terms of our fight or flight response. In real terms, it's kept our species alive for thousands of years. Perceived fears, things based on our imagination or based on information loaded into our subconscious memory that is very often not accurate and can be negative. However, unfortunately our instinctive responses do not differentiate between what is real and what is perceived, particularly when we get an intuitive early warning feeling that is hard to tangibly measure.

There are many examples of this but here is one simple one: *If you've just watched a scary movie and your subconscious is primed with the information from that movie, it's quite likely that after that movie your senses will be heightened and you will notice that things that never worried you before, for example a dark passage or a sudden noise, may, all of the sudden trigger a pretty drastic fear based response.* This response is not necessarily linked to a higher threat level or a real threat, but is rather because you've primed your subconscious with this information based on the movie you just watched. i.e. the threat is totally perceived with no real basis for feeling this way other than the way you have been primed based on the information you have just exposed yourself to in the movie.

---

[2] "Fear – The Friend of Exceptional People". Geoff Thompson. July 2001. Retrieved 2008-01-27.

It's of major importance that we need to consider that everything we experience, see, hear, touch, talk about, etc. is stored in our subconscious memory. Therefore, if you load your subconscious memory with preconceived ideas or inaccurate perceptions, it's quite likely that your intuition may be triggered based on some of these ideas or perceptions, which may or may not be accurate. As I'm not currently face to face with you, nor am I your psychologist, guidance counselor, or confidante, it is not possible for me to personally work out with you what your real fears and what your perceived fears are. I would however, encourage you to undertake the activity of your own accord simply because if you're able to eliminate perceived fear, you know that when your intuition kicks in, it's kicking in based on a real fear and not perception. Therefore, your reactions are more easily justified and we can eliminate unnecessary paranoia and anxiety. Whilst drawing from the research of experts such as Daniel Kahneman[3] in terms of our two distinct systems – our intuitive mind (System 1) and our cognitive mind (System 2) showing that in many cases with time for analysis, we make better decisions. The cognitive processes take too long and in a critical life or death situation, will likely be overruled by our instinctive and emotional responses, governed by our intuitive mind. Therefore, eliminating inaccuracies and ineffective preconceptions creates a more reliable instinctive response capability.

Generally speaking, we have found that women are more likely to trust their intuition and listen to gut feeling based on pure emotive content than men, who seem to want active and accurate proof before reacting or responding to something in their environment. Our goal should be that regardless of our predisposition, to trust emotion over factual evidence, we should learn to trust our intuition implicitly when it comes to urgent safety decisions that need to be made. Let's examine this further and take a random figure to support this statement. Let's say that your intuitive early warning responses were wrong 50% of the

---

[3]I highly recommend that if you are interested in learning to make better decision that you read Daniel Kahneman's excellent book – **Thinking, Fast and Slow**.

GENERALLY SPEAKING, WE HAVE FOUND THAT WOMEN ARE MORE LIKELY TO TRUST THEIR INTUITION AND LISTEN TO GUT FEELING BASED ON PURE EMOTIVE CONTENT THAN MEN, WHO SEEM TO WANT ACTIVE AND ACCURATE PROOF BEFORE REACTING OR RESPONDING TO SOMETHING IN THEIR ENVIRONMENT.

time, it means the other 50% of the time your intuitive response is effectively acting as your body's early warning defense mechanism and is structured in such a way that it may very well protect you and keep you safe. Even if you were wrong 50% of the time, the likelihood is in that 50%, you may only land up adding minor inconvenience, such as a longer walk or a longer commute, or you land up offending somebody by being rude. In either case, I'm sure most of you will agree that it would be better to be considered rude than get attacked? I am sure you agree it would be better to be slightly late than to be assaulted? Trusting your intuition as a wonderful gift that could enhance your safety tremendously if primed and honed correctly is the basis for applying proactive awareness skills and building enhanced instinctive safety capabilities.

Learning to raise and lower awareness

Once we understand how intuition works and we understand our base priming and conditioning, the next step is to understand how to raise and lower our awareness effectively. The problem we have is that we only have a very limited amount of laser-like focus in any given period of time. This level of focus is used up when we need to concentrate on tasks every day. In order to understand the need to raise and lower awareness, we need to accept the fact that we have limits to our ability to multitask, as well as to focus on a specific issue for an extended period of time.

If we borrow from the field of sports psychology and look at the way that most athletes perform, we see that some of the athletes in games that may take an extended period of time, such as cricket or baseball, who are either getting pitched or bowled to, have periods of intense focus as well as time for recovery and regrouping. The athletes that tend to perform the best in these type of activities, are the ones that are able to have laser-like focus when they're on pitch or on bat but then straightaway switch it off and wind their awareness down when they have a gap. This skill set is so important for them because it's estimated that we only have roughly about 30 minutes of intense focus in any given 10 to 12-hour period. Obviously, this may differ from person to person but creates a base starting point for us. Let's assume that a player used up their limited laser-like focus in the first 30 minutes of the game, they are then unlikely to perform very well for the balance. Similarly, for you and I, if we work through our laser-like focus in a very quick period of time based on inaccurate perceptions of what may go wrong, we're now, in essence, running on zero. It's at this point that feelings of stress, anxiety and paranoia develop.

In very real terms, paranoia, stress and anxiety make you less aware and in fact, make you an easier target and a more likely victim for criminals or people with ill intent. Running on an empty 'focus tank' also obviously has a massive effect on the quality of life and the way you live your life. In extreme circumstances, it could even lead to signs and symptoms very similar to post-traumatic stress disorder (PTSD). It's truly to your advantage to learn to raise and lower your

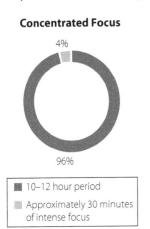

Concentrated Focus

4%

96%

- 10–12 hour period
- Approximately 30 minutes of intense focus

awareness in a practical manner. One of the tools that helps us achieve this balance is the use of color code systems.

Color codes are often attributed to the late Jeff Cooper,[4] who developed

Colour Codes of Awareness

WHITE	YELLOW	ORANGE	RED
Relaxed unaware unprepared	Relaxed alert (non-specific)	Alert (specific)	Fight: (mental trigger)

a color code system to be applied in the way soldiers and other sheepdogs prepared for battlefield encounters. This has been changed, adapted and modified in many ways, but is still a very useful tool. A basic overarching understanding of color codes is very useful in terms of teaching us when to raise or lower our awareness. In terms of looking at how we do this, we should look at the base colors. The system consists of five colors. The first color, white, represents a state of absolute peace or zero threat. Yellow represents a state of basic awareness. Orange is a heightened state of awareness and preparation for response. Red is a required response or action, which may relate to an attack situation or incident actually occurring.

The last color, Black,[5] usually refers to a state of war, where you need to kill before being killed. For most everyday people, who do not serve in the police or military or higher security environments, black is not an everyday occurrence and as such, it is not normally included in the color codes. It should be remembered that even when we go into color White, for example when we're in our own home, we usually have our doors locked; we might have burglar alarms, dogs or other early warning or protective systems which would alert us to something suspicious. This

---

[4]For more information see: Cooper, J. (2006). *Principles of Personal Defense*, Paladin Press, Boulder, Colorado – first published in 1972.

[5]Note: the original colour codes did not have black, it was added by another expert Massad Ayoob and is generally now an acknowledged addition.

The Dynamics of Real-World Violence with Color Codes

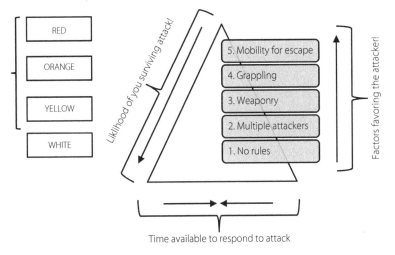

Time available to respond to attack

serves as a good example of when an environment is not threatening, and as such, enables us to let our awareness down to the lowest level. The reality is that if we carry on and go about our everyday life in color white, it's not just a security issue, it could be potentially very dangerous for you in terms of unnecessary exposure to a wide range of other hazards and risks. Let's now add this color-code system to the earlier figure we used. We can interpret it as follows: The truth is we are hardly ever completely safe when out and about, living your life (which is a pre-requisite for being in condition *White*). Therefore, we leave that out of the equation. Research has shown that you can be in condition *Yellow* 24/7 without risk of burnout. It is a general state of awareness. The earlier we pick up the warning signs of an imminent threat or attack (condition *Yellow*), the more time (even if it's milliseconds) you will have to prepare for whatever is coming (condition *Orange*). This happens on a conscious and subconscious level. Finally, by the time the actual confrontation happens, you will have made the decision to either avoid the situation by fleeing (the preferred option), or fight (an absolute last resort) – condition *Red*. Understanding and applying the color code system actually improves your chances of survival exponentially! Unfortunately, the converse is also true. If you're caught napping in condition *White* and an attack is initiated against you, you will immediately move to condition *Red*, where all the factors favoring the attackers are in play against you, and you've had no opportunity to prepare at all.

This sort of Color Code system is not unique. Think of the basis for traffic laws and safe driving requirements. A basic color-code system is applied to the way traffic lights work. For example, when it's green, you can proceed because it's safe. Red means it is not safe for you to proceed. Orange or amber signals that you can proceed with caution or prepare to stop. The general awareness color codes work very much the same way. They serve as a base point for you to be able to understand threats, risks and hazards happening around you and to ensure that your level of awareness is in line with your environment and the people there.

For example: *Let's imagine you're walking down the road minding your own business. I think we would all agree you should be in color yellow. You see two suspicious looking men rushing towards you. Having identified the potential threat, you proactively cross the road. As you take action, you simultaneously go from yellow to orange, preparing yourself for something a little bit more in case it is required. Let's say the two suspicious men don't follow you across the road, you could then revert back to yellow and carry on with your day. However, if they do cross the road and attempt to go after you, you'd have to move into red and either run or fight.* **There can be little doubt that it is easier to move to action in a graduated approach then to have to panic and respond.**

HAVING A METHOD TO RAISE AND LOWER OUR AWARENESS IS CRITICALLY IMPORTANT.

In terms of being able to ration that very short and critical amount of intense focus we have every day in a practical way – having a method to raise and lower our awareness is critically important. By learning to align our level of awareness to the actual threats and issues around you, you should be able to perform more effectively. Not applying a method to raise and lower awareness could mean that you just land up worrying about things that are not worth worrying about or being distracted by things that may not actually pose a threat and potentially exposing yourself not only to a higher level of vulnerability to attack, but also to negative health issues based on stress and anxiety.

Now that we've covered three fundamental concepts of our awareness toolbox, namely baselining, intuition and color codes, we can move on to the applied observational aspects. The ability to actually assess and evaluate what is happening around you will be covered in the next section, but the core application of intuitive understanding and the application of color codes forms the basis to examine our next critical tool.

What to look for and how to prepare – the '3PC-S approach'

As I've already stated, over the years we've trained thousands of security professionals from all over the globe. When we started doing this about 20 years ago, we encountered intense frustration. We found that seasoned security professionals, whether they were from private security, policing or military backgrounds, seemed to have developed an inbuilt or intuitive system for being able to determine if an environment was safe or if the people there would be up to no good, or potentially be totally innocent and not pose a threat. This capability, is without doubt, a crucial skills set since if we don't know how to tell if our environment is safe or not, how would we know which color code we should be in?

In order to address the dilemma of how to provide new recruits with the knowledge and skills exhibited by seasoned veterans, we needed to understand what these professionals do. We were under pressure to try and shorten the time for new recruits to become more effective, so we embarked on a basic research process and interviewed as many of these professionals as possible. Initially, this was a frustrating process as many of these professionals simply highlighted that they '*don't know how they know*' when something was a threat or not or they didn't quite know '*how they knew somebody would be taking a negative action or an attack stance' – these were just instinctive and natural pieces of knowledge for them.* As we spoke to more and more people, it became clear that these abilities were simply the evolution of decades of experience, which had taught them how humans behave and what the triggers to potentially negative action related to differing environmental contexts are.

In interviewing these professionals, we came up with a wide range of relevant data. This data was then correlated into three key points so that it could be systemized and passed onto new recruits. We called the system the 'Three Point Check System' or 3PC-S for short. This system has been taught to thousands of people both everyday civilians and security professionals as, very early, it became clear to us that the same tool used by security professionals could be useful to the normal everyday person, it just needed a bit of contextualization. The 3PC-S provides the missing piece required to complete our awareness tool box which already contains the tools of baselining, intuition and color codes.

In practical terms, the 3PC-S is a system that will tell you whether the environment you're in is safe based on the surroundings, the people there and what's happening at the time. From your perspective, in terms of how to apply the 3PC-S, with a bit of practice this entire system should only take you three to four seconds, and with more practice it should become habitual – something that you do all the time without thinking, just like the experts do. In fact, I guarantee that you do many of the aspects that make up the 3PC-S already without thinking, you just may not have put them together.

If we simply look at what you do when you decide you are going to cross a busy street – the process of looking left and right and determining when it is safe to proceed can be made very complicated or very simple. This process of basic road safety may be interpreted as what safety professionals may call *'a job safety analysis'* or; what risk professionals may call a *'complex risk analysis'* or even what security professionals may call *'a threat assessment'*. In reality, this process becomes an inbuilt, taught behavioral skill based on years of training and rehearsal. The instinctive capability developed to check whether it is safe to cross

IN PRACTICAL TERMS, THE 3PC-S IS A SYSTEM THAT WILL TELL YOU WHETHER THE ENVIRONMENT YOU'RE IN IS SAFE BASED ON THE SURROUNDINGS, THE PEOPLE THERE AND WHAT'S HAPPENING AT THE TIME.

the road, is where we'd like to get to with our scanning and observational capabilities, and is the core goal in terms of a developing the habitual use of the 3PC-S.

So, what are the key aspects of the 3PC-S? The very first point of the 3PC-S is to equip you with the ability to scan your environment. Your environment may be defined as *anything around you at any given time*. For example, if I'm driving on a freeway, the environment is the road and the cars around me. If I'm walking down the street, it is the surroundings of the street itself and the buildings around me. How we assess our environment in a generic way, no matter what it is, enables us to assess a baseline for safety and understanding of potential threats, hazards or risks. To be more thorough we further subdivide the environment into three subcategories.

The starting point upon which most security professionals hinge their situational assessments on is understanding the basic placement and location of **exits, entrances, escape routes and hiding places**. In other words, **where could you get out from if something went wrong, or where would people with ill intent be coming in from? Where could you hide if things went wrong or where would potential assailants wanting to attack me be hiding?**

Once you understand these base points, you are able to start understanding the risks that your environment may harbor… As a practical example, *think of a shopping mall or place you go too often. Have you really paid attention to where the fire escapes are?* Have you taken into consideration that they've been put there for a reason? In fact, many people who've responded in active shooter situations and have survived, are people who knew secondary escape and access points and had pre-planned and imprinted in their subconscious memory their locations so that they could respond reflexively and utilize them under emergency conditions.

The second point in terms of scanning your environment is to be able to identify objects or items that seem suspicious and have a basic under-standing of the structural aspects and obstacles around you. This is criti-cally important. You do not have to know from an engineering perspective exactly *how many bricks are in the wall or exactly how many walls are in a building,* but **you should know that if you had to try and reach a hid-ing place or run to an exit, whether there are structures or obstacles that could get in your way or hinder you**. You would like to know if you had to, for example, *drive over a pavement because somebody was following you, whether or not it was too high for your vehicle to ramp over it if you needed to, etc.* Considering the thousands of people we have trained and interviewed, many people who shared information on vehicle carjacking's who had successfully identified the threat early on and tried to drive away, had actually driven into parked cars or other obstacles like trees because of their lack of structural awareness or obstacle identification.

The last point to be covered under the 3PC-S primary heading of Environment, is what we refer to as **improvised weapons and defen-sive objects**. Improvised weapons refer to anything in your environ-ment that an attacker could use to harm you with. Conversely, defensive objects refer to anything in your environment that you could use to defend yourself with. In many situations, these are the same items and are truly only limited by your, or the attackers' ability to improvise and utilize such items in the immediate environment to inflict harm.

In terms of understanding the basis of core defensive objects and tools, we may not often think about parked cars, walls or the floor as something that we could use to help defend ourselves with, but **the measure of a good defensive tool is whether it gives you an advan-tage when you are attacked or not**. If it is something that would cause significant harm to your attacker, and using it has more benefit than not, then it's probably a good idea to identify it ahead of time. Think back to what we discussed in the principles of violence where most fights land up on the ground. If you go down to the ground, where there could be glass and tar, you may get hurt just by being on the ground itself. Conversely, if you're able to use it as a defensive item, then it may help you in terms of defending yourself against a bigger, stronger, more aggressive attacker, for example throwing your attacker onto the ground so he hurts himself.

When faced by an attacker, simply understanding that a pen in your hand may be a critical survival resource and an amazing defensive tool could help you prepare and predict possible actions or even deter an attacker based on you demonstrating more confidence. Similarly, understanding that criminals may utilize any object around them to inflict harm on you when they attack you, is a useful success point from the perspective of assessing whether your environment is safe or not. In certain environments, we should take into account the fact that it may not just be improvised weapons, but actual weapons used, such as firearms that may be all too readily available. This means that they may be used either offensively, i.e. against you, or defensively, by you or others to protect yourself and others. As previously mentioned the ability to utilize a tool dramatically improves our chances of defending against it which when it comes to lethal weapons – such as firearms, may be lifesaving knowledge.

In summary, the first point of the 3PC-S focuses on scanning our environment. Under this heading, first and foremost, we **assess entrances, exits, escape routes and hiding places. Secondly, we assess Suspicious items, Structural aspects and Obstacles**. Lastly, we assess **improvised weapons and defensive tools**. Once we've completed our environmental scan, we should be able to determine whether the environment itself is safe or not. However, the reality is that with the exception of natural disasters or major catastrophic events such as a building collapse, most environmental threats are comparatively easy to predict because of their comparatively slow action time. For example, *imagine you walk into a building and you have to go to the third floor. As you walk in you look at the elevator in the building and it looks like it was well over*

100 years old and very rickety and shaky. I am sure you, like most of us, would identify this as a hazard and rather make use of the stairs. As another example, *if you walk into a restaurant, sit down on a chair and feel that this chair is very rickety and shaky, in all likelihood, you would then change chairs.* As we can see, it is usually not pure environmental risk that is our personal safety concern but a combination of the environmental aspects together with the people in the given environment that truly poses the larger potential risk.

This brings us to the second point in the 3PC-S – people. This core skill set centers around how we actually assess people from a threat and vulnerability perspective? As with our environmental assessment we need to break down the way we assess people into a further three sub-aspects. In the first instance, **we generally assess most people based on their appearance**. What do they look like? Appearance can be divided into many different aspects. From an observational perspective, we tend to focus on things we like to look at first and usually ignore what we don't like to look at. With discipline we can improve this skill by following the way we scan naturally – from most obvious item to least or from most interesting to least interesting and enhancing it. Clothing is the first aspect of assessment. Depending on where you live, people are often covered with clothing to differing degrees but they usually wear something. Most of us already have this inbuilt assessment process but we often assess appearance based on what we perceive to be fashionable or attractive not necessarily giving any consideration to security. If we try and take our existing skills to the next level and also assess appearance based on whether the person could they be concealing weaponry or whether they are dressed in such a way that they would be breaking up the shape of their face, via wearing a cap and sunglasses, we could potentially also gain some security foresight and benefit.

In terms of assessing people, we tend to run a process, which happens very quickly, where we first assess clothing, then we quickly assess gender, race, size etc. Other aspects related to the way the person looks usually get taken into consideration after these early identifiers and include aspects such as tattoos or jewelry. The reality is that we tend to focus on looking at things we like to look at and don't look at things we don't like to look at, which is very often why we miss appearance based early warning indicators. With a bit of discipline and practice this is easily overcome.

However, even if you become an expert in assessing people risk based on appearance, the difficulty we have, is that if appearance alone were enough to determine threatening intent, the police could just arrest people for the way they look and we would never have crime. We know that the seasoned criminal or terrorist is usually very effective at blending into their environment. Once we understand and accept this reality, we understand that assessing on appearance alone is simply not good enough, we need to look at the next level of assessing potentially risky people.

The next level refers to the process of **assessing peoples' attitude, behavior and body language**. Attitude generally refers to the way a person interacts with their environment from a holistic perspective. For example, *are they behaving in a way that seems to be in concert with everyone else around them or is their behavior a little out of the ordinary?* In terms of body language, *are there non-verbal communicative cues, things that don't seem to be normal, do they seem to be a little off-center?* Some examples of this could include *people who are perhaps sitting in a corner, avoiding eye contact, sweating profusely and every now and again looking twitchy or anxious. If everybody else around them seems to be having a good time, this is obviously an indicator of potential threatening behavior.*

There are many circumstances where we need to assess behavior. As another example, *if you walk into a bar and you identify a large group of rowdy tattooed men wearing leathers, chains, and being very loud and raucous,* most people would identify this as a potential threat and generally seek to avoid them, but conversely, we might not necessarily notice the person previously described sitting in the corner, observing what is happening displaying significant nervous behavior. Who may actually be a bigger threat to you? Well, that depends on all of the variables. The reality is that if you haven't been sufficiently aware to pick up both levels of threat, you are significantly vulnerable. Once we have assessed people based on Appearance, Attitude, Behavior and Body language we have gathered a lot of potential data but we still need to look at one last aspect.

The last aspect in terms of assessing people is what we refer to as grouping. Very few criminals act alone. It's important for us to understand how to identify grouping structures because that tells us the likelihood of potential attack and where that attack may actually manifest from. When we understand the concept of grouping, it is easier to avoid a situation. As an example of how grouping may work, *imagine you're walking into a bank and outside the bank there is a very suspicious looking person leaning against the door. He has a hat pulled really low. He's doing his very best to avoid eye contact while he has his hands in his pocket. You think to yourself as you walk past, this guy seems a little suspicious. You proceed into the bank and while you are waiting in line to see one of the tellers, there is somebody in front of you with the exact same profile. This person and the person outside, every now and again, lock eyes and look at each other for a split second before breaking contact.* This information significantly changes the risk profile of where you are, it tells you that in all likelihood you've gone from one suspicious guy loitering outside the bank to an imminent bank robbery and should be a significant warning indicator for you to communicate what you have seen and leave – not necessarily in that order.

In summary, looking at the second point of the 3PC-S, if we look at people, the ways to assess them in terms of them being a potential threat include looking at appearance as a starting point and whether from a security perspective, could they be concealing anything that could cause harm? Are they trying to cover up the way they look or are they simply trying too hard to blend in? The next aspect of people assessment is looking at attitude, behavior and body language. Trying to identify whether the way people are behaving is inconsistent or seems slightly out of place, considering everything else that is happening around you, is an important aspect. Lastly, the third consideration when evaluating people is to assess grouping – are there obvious groups that may pose a threat or are there groups of people that appear to be unrelated yet seem to exhibit similar types of suspicious behavior?

Once you've put this all together, assessed the environment and assessed the people there, you can then move on to the **last aspect of the 3PC-S which is coming up with a plan**. We call this phase the **Planned Incident Action (PIA) or 'What if' phase**. The 3PC-S is a three out of three thing, you don't get good grade for getting only part of it right, let's say you do well and can tick off the first checkpoint – assessing the environment. You also successfully apply the second – assessing people. It does not help that you get the first two right and identify someone acting suspiciously in your environment, but are not able to come up with a basic reaction plan. A good plan could be very simple but it is important to follow through and think about what you would actually do if something bad happened based on the information you have gathered in phase one and two of the 3PC-S. This aspect will be elaborated on in more detail in the coming chapters but at the very least, wherever you are, you want to come up with three base levels of

3 Point Check System (3PC-S):

1. **P**lace/Environment
   a. Entrances, exits, escape routes, hiding places
   b. Suspicious items, Obstacles & Structural aspects
   c. Improvised weaponry & defensive tools

2. **P**eople
   a. Appearance
   b. Attitude, Behavior, Body language
   c. Grouping

3. **P**lanned Incident Actions (PIA's) & **C**ontingency planning
   a. Run, Hide or Fight – Communicate response

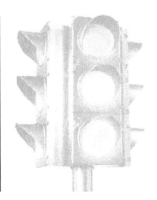

planning based on a **run, hide** and as a last resort, **fight** methodology. In other words, you should know where you go to escape and how you could escape if you had to run. If you had to hide, you should understand where you could hide in a place that could provide cover and concealment (Cover and Concealment will be discussed in the Chapter on Taking Action). Lastly, by assessing and identifying improvised weapons and defensive tools, you would have, at the very least, mapped out a basic plan that would allow you, in the worst-case scenario, to defend yourself having the knowledge of what could be used against you or what you could use to protect yourself.

Chapter summary

In summary, when we assess awareness, we look at three core concepts that make up our awareness tool box. These three tools and skillsets are:

1. Understanding the importance of base lining
2. Understanding and trusting our intuition
3. Understanding how to raise and lower our awareness using color codes
4. Understanding how to apply observational techniques – applying the 3PC-S

Once you're able to put these tools together, you should have a robust base not just to apply but to effectively manage awareness. Applied awareness should enable you to focus effectively and not be distracted by what you may perceive as relevant, based on incorrect programming. We also know that paranoia is as negative as not being alert at all. As such, we should strive to find the balance between being aware, based on the requirements of our environment and the people around us, so that we can mitigate and manage anxiety and stress and perform effectively. The goal should be to make the toolbox a habit. The challenge for you is very simple. We have found that applying the 3PC-S takes around 3–5 seconds for people who are new to it. If you are willing to sacrifice just 5 minutes of your time over the next 21 days, you could go a long way towards making these skills habitual and then it's easy because you will apply the system without even thinking about it. Basically, you need to allocate 15 seconds a day for the next twenty-one days to conduct a 3PC-S in different environments at least 3 times each day. That's it – simply doing this is a really easy way to build your awareness skills with the minimum amount of hassle – good luck! The next chapter will focus on the way we analyze and interpret information to determine how we should act in different situations.

CHAPTER 4

Working Out What to Do...

The process of assessment

Once you have gained the confidence to apply the awareness toolbox covered in the last chapter and you can scan your environment effectively, you need to ensure that you can effectively assess what is happening and forecast what may happen. We need to be able to make sure that our baselining combined with our ability to really assess what is likely to happen and what may be the impact or consequence of what may happen, is in place. We don't want to get caught in the position where our initial awareness levels are very effective, but our assessments are all wrong. In other words, we are able to gather the relevant information but we don't sort it and analyze it effectively so we either over or under react or even worse fail to act if necessary... The concept of Dynamic Risk Equilibrium (DRE) as applied to assessment can be highlighted if we focus on issues that, whilst having noticed them, they have a very small likelihood of actually occurring. Conversely, we don't want to miss something that may have a small likelihood of occurring, but should it occur, have a massive consequence or impact. In other words, we would like to ensure we assess effectively but strive to ensure we are not being paranoid nor demonstrating denial or bias that may have a negative effect on our ability to analyze and forecast.

In terms of basic risk management, the core functions of assessing the likelihood of an incident or an event and the consequence of that event are the key building blocks for trying to assess whether or not the said issue is something that needs to be managed or not. From your perspective as an individual trying to ensure that you and your family stay safe and enjoy a great quality of life, the ability to come up with an accurate assessment is an important factor. This is primarily because when we take into account the limited amount of effort and energy you may be willing to allocate to your own personal safety and wellbeing, it is important to expend it in the best possible manner you can.

THE CORE FUNCTIONS OF ASSESSING THE LIKELIHOOD OF AN INCIDENT OR AN EVENT AND THE CONSEQUENCE OF THAT EVENT ARE THE KEY BUILDING BLOCKS FOR TRYING TO ASSESS WHETHER THE SAID ISSUE IS SOMETHING THAT NEEDS TO BE MANAGED OR NOT.

In order to ensure we get on top of this, we need to dig a bit deeper. We need to look at further variables and issues that apply to our safety and our ability to mitigate the likelihood of bad things happening. Once your awareness toolbox is in place, we need to understand that the first thing that every single crime or terrorist attack has in common is that it is always preceded by a process of victim selection and an attacker ritual. No matter how random an attack may seem, there is always a process through which a criminal or a terrorist would determine what target they will attack and how they plan to attack it. This process is sometimes referred to as the 'rational model of criminal behavior', where criminals weigh up the risk vs reward of committing a certain act on a said target. Without trying to over simplify a complex subject, in terms of attacker ritual and victim selection, it is important to understand that most criminals choose their target based on what they might get out of it, combined with the likelihood of them successfully perpetrating their crime, i.e. not getting caught.

In the mind of a criminal

Whilst a basic risk vs reward equation is attractive, unfortunately we have to also factor in the reality that many criminals and terrorist don't make decisions based on a rational mindset. They may be high on some sort of drugs or not thinking rationally because of a possible mental disorder. Furthermore, we should not discount the realities of religious or ideological persuasion, which may actually warp somebody's thought processes to the point where they actually believe that extreme acts of violence such as blowing up a school bus full of children is a good idea. From your perspective, in terms of assessing the likelihood of something occurring, the starting point is understanding that not all people view the world through the same eyes as you do. Just because you hold a certain perspective and respect for human rights, a code of morality and the rule of law, doesn't necessarily mean that criminals and terrorists do. In fact, the reality is that they usually don't see things from this sort of perspective at all and are usually able to justify their own actions in the belief that what they are doing is right based on their belief and/or personal circumstances.

> MOST CRIMINALS CHOOSE THEIR TARGET BASED ON WHAT THEY MIGHT GET OUT OF IT, COMBINED WITH THE LIKELIHOOD OF THEM SUCCESSFULLY PERPETRATING THEIR CRIME, I.E. NOT GETTING CAUGHT.

Building on this reality, if we look at the way criminals commit crimes and why they commit crimes, motivations may be based on reward aspects that are not as simple as basic financial returns such as social motives, ideological motives or even psychological issues such as the behavior exhibited by sociopaths and psychopaths. As you can see, these examples can be based on quite complex motives and very often, these motives are way more than just simple reward. The perceived reward itself may also be complex from an attacker's perspective for example rewards could include, social acceptance, where criminals commit crimes because they want to be accepted by their peers. Motives may be based on upbringing and ideology, where the attacker believes people who do not think the same as they do, deserve to be harmed or forced into changing their thoughts and behaviors. Without over thinking motive and making sure we focus on your own span of control – let's bring it back to a very simple risk vs reward equation in terms of you, as a victim, having something that they want. Accepting that it is not always about securing cash or assets as the motive for committing crime, helps us understand that it may be based on a psychological issue where, for example, many rapists have been diagnosed with disorders which have shown that they committed these offenses not for sexual deviancy reasons, but more for empowerment reasons and for reasons of wanting to prove their own manhood to themselves.

Despite all of these wonderful criminological and societal views, the long and the short of this assessment process is trying to evaluate whether somebody will hurt you, how will they hurt you, where are they likely to attack you, what the impact of that attack would be and what you can do to minimize the likelihood of the said attack from occurring at all. In fact, we need to try and assess whether it's something that you should be putting time, effort and energy into at all.

It is useful to analyze the concepts of attacker ritual and victim selection for numerous reasons, but primarily because if we can gain a peek into the mind of our opposition, we can figure out how to stop them. As a starting point on the journey to try and understand why people do bad things, I would like to run you through a basic visualization exercise.

Start of visualization exercise:

As you read this I would like you to imagine that you are in a third-world country. Imagine you've grown up in this country. You had a basic job and you were making just enough to look after your family. For whatever reason you've lost your job, you've now been living on the streets with your family for a few days, begging for food, begging for money. You and your family are absolutely starving. You see a wealthy Western tourist walk past you with a pocket full of cash. What goes through your mind as you see someone who has something you desperately need, walk past you?

In a normal state of mind, you may not consider taking the money, but if you were really in a position where you and your family were starving, you would probably think, right, what would be the harm to that person, if I get to eat and feed my family. You may consider trying to rob the person.

Most people would start off with a basic pickpocket type of crime with a simplistic approach, which would be along the lines of maybe bumping into the person and trying to pick their pocket or distracting them for the same purpose. Let's say that you attempt to pull this off and as you grab for the wallet, this person turns around and assaults you. You're now in a position where you're tired, cold, hungry and in pain...

Despite this failure, you are likely to reevaluate the way that you decide to commit such a crime – again, bearing in mind that you're still hungry and cold and need to feed your family.

Perhaps you think of a different strategy and your strategy might be to try to sneak up on the person and strike them in the back of the head and then while they're distracted and in pain, you grab the money and run away. You implement this and find it to be quite effective!

Onto the next victim... You see an old lady walking down the road, wearing lots of gold jewelry. You think to yourself, what a great opportunity. I don't even have to hit her that hard. As you walk up to assault her, you neglect to see that she has two six-foot-six men standing behind her, who are actually her sons. They throw you down on the ground and apply instant street justice. You're once again tired, hungry and in pain.

You would now most likely rethink your strategy and decide, right, I need to look at a better place to hunt, a place that enables me to blend in and evaluate my surroundings better. You may also look at how you select a victim. You might look to choose somebody who we would generally refer to as an 'easy target'. An easy target being somebody who we could easily overpower, somebody distracted and unaware and somebody who obviously had whatever we were after, in this case, cash. You might also consider actually getting a weapon, perhaps for example, stealing a knife from a local restaurant. Let's say you do so. With your new-found approach and enhanced strategies, which incorporate a better planning and victim selection process as well as using a knife, threatening the person, picking a better place, picking easier targets, you find thing go much smoother for you. In fact, you find that these aspects combine as very effective 'business development tools' which directly result in a lower risk level for you and a greater return.

Let's imagine that using all of your new strategies and tools, you find somebody walking down the street and you think to yourself, this is going to be a good opportunity. You wave your knife in front of their face, but unfortunately, they don't respond in the manner you thought and unlike in the movies, they don't immediately stop and give up. They continue to fight back and defend themselves despite the fact that you are cutting them – you're now back at the start again, tired, cold, hungry and in pain.

In terms of managing the risk, you may now look at other options such as looking to get people to help you. Assessing options such as – Could I form a gang to commit these crimes? Could I potentially get another weapon, like a firearm? You may also consider upping your use of force, in which case if a potential victim that you were targeting even resisted at all, you may rapidly resort to violence.

End of visualization exercise.

This visualization exercise highlights a few things but primarily illustrates what criminologists sometimes as refer to as the 'logical progression of violent crime' whereby the majority of criminals don't actually use violence as a tool for self-pleasure or gratification. They simply use it as a tool because it gets better results. Based on this model, we can begin to understand and assess that if potential attackers or criminals are given a fair risk vs reward ratio, and are not given a reason to utilize violence as a tool, they may not resort to high levels of violence. In terms of these type of attackers, cooperation is usually the most effective survival action if you were not able to prevent or avoid an attack its entirety.

Whilst understanding the logical progression of violent crime is a good starting point, let's look at it from another perspective. People with extreme ideological or religious persuasions that dictate the use of violence to further their purposes; people who might have grown up in war-torn countries; or – as we mentioned earlier – people who have grown up as child soldiers with no moral compass; people who have grown up in an environment where 'might literally makes right ', may use violence not really as a tool to get better results,

> IN MOST CASES, IF POTENTIAL ATTACKERS OR CRIMINALS ARE GIVEN A FAIR RISK VS REWARD RATIO, AND ARE NOT GIVEN A REASON TO UTILIZE VIOLENCE AS A TOOL, THEY MAY NOT RESORT TO HIGH LEVELS OF VIOLENCE. IN TERMS OF THESE TYPE OF ATTACKERS, COOPERATION IS USUALLY THE MOST EFFECTIVE SURVIVAL ACTION IF AVOIDANCE COULD NOT BE ACHIEVED.

but simply because it's part of their everyday life. For people like this using violence, hurting and even killing people is just another action.

There are many places in the world where the value of life or the value of somebody's wellbeing is not measured by some sort of moralistic or legalistic output, but may be measured quite literally by the cost of a cell phone or a watch. While we may not agree with it, we need to acknowledge this reality, otherwise we cannot effectively provide a base for accurate assessment in terms of how likely an incident is to occur, and how serious the consequences may be. This is further complicated if we are dealing with people who may be high on drugs or mentally unstable.

Leading on from an understanding of these two perspectives – using violence as a tool (Type 1) or using violence based on ideological, cultural desensitization, substance abuse or mental instability (Type 2) – leads us to a critical output, namely whether we can simply look at people and assess whether they would commit violent crime, and whether they would be a person who would use violence as a tool to get better results (Type 1), or whether they are somebody who would just as easily kill you without blinking an eye (Type 2). Because it is impossible to assess type 1 vs type 2 motives at a glance, unfortunately, when it comes to personal safety, we often must take a very conservative view, which usually involves looking at a worst-case scenario of what may happen to you and this means when in doubt we have to assume that a person willing to use violence may be Type 2. Even if you feel that the person seems to be a Type 1 motivated, if we honestly believe that somebody may be in a position to harm us, and has the intent and belief to do so, it's always better to err on the side of caution in assessing the situation.

IT'S IMPORTANT TO UNDERSTAND THAT THE OBJECTIVE IS QUITE LITERALLY TO TURN OURSELVES INTO A HARD TARGET, A TARGET THAT AN ATTACKER WOULD NOT SELECT.

We should make sure that when we conduct our basic process of assessing the who, what, when, where, how and why of the way an attacker may select us, or our house, or our family, or our work place as a valid target, we must take into cognizance that their state of mind may not be that of a sane or a rational person. This forms the core starting point for the way we should assess the likelihood and consequences of an attack. It's important to understand that the objective is quite literally to turn ourselves into a hard target, a target that an attacker would not select. At the end of the day, while ideologically we should strive for a safer society, this may not be within our power to achieve. A more achievable goal may simply be to make you, your workplace, your family and your home, hard targets so that an attacker would prefer to pick on somebody else. Whilst it is not always palatable to try and think like a criminal or terrorist, if you really try to do so, it is not too hard to apply a rational approach and try and work out the who, what, when, why and how of a potential attack. This should enable us to prevent or avoid 90% of potential incidents – simply by being an unpalatable target.

The other 10% comes from non-rational attackers who are unpredictable or highly professional attackers who may have extensive resources to be able to overcome your preventative methodologies.

In the next section, we will discuss in detail what may make you a hard or an unattractive target so that hopefully, somebody with ill intent would simply move on and pick another target.

Target hardening: how to transform yourself into a hard target

In the previous section, we focused quite a lot on the reality of assessment and trying to understand the way that criminals, terrorists or people who could harm us make decisions, so that we are able to determine what we need to do to ensure that we are not selected as the target as well as how to conduct ourselves in the correct manner so as to get out of a negative situation, should we land in it.

The reality, unfortunately, is that attacks are very dynamic. Your ability to assess a situation and assess the full consequences of action or inaction can come down to a timeframe of around 0.3 of a second. In 0.3 of a second, it would literally be impossible to work out all the consequences of whatever action you may want to perform or even to consider whether you should do anything at all. Therefore, trying to determine in advance what you would, or wouldn't do, is a critical aspect in terms of preparation and target hardening. Obviously, our goal should be centered around

> TRYING TO DETERMINE IN ADVANCE WHAT YOU WOULD, OR WOULDN'T DO, IS A CRITICAL ASPECT IN TERMS OF PREPARATION AND TARGET HARDENING.

focusing on the avoidance and prevention of crime, violence and terrorist attacks as opposed to focusing on the coping or management of situations should they occur.

As previously mentioned, roughly 80% of your time, effort and energy – which may not be much time at all – should be spent on focusing on what we do to prevent these things from happening. The other 20% could be spent on what we focus on doing should these things actually happen, and how we would respond, recover and get back to enjoying a quality of life after an event occurs.

We could use the *Pareto Principle* (as previously discussed) to further illustrate this point. Determine the top 20% of things in your life you can focus on with regards to avoidance and prevention of becoming a victim of crime or terrorism. This could be done by asking yourself some questions, e.g.

- Are there any habits in my life that are making me a soft target?
- Am I aware of the crime statistics for the area I'm living in?
- Do I know who to contact in case of emergency?
- Am I applying basic Cyber Security when online?
- Etc.

Then focus 80% of your time, effort and energy on that 20%. This will result in an 80% return on investment, in other words theoretically there would be an 80% less chance of you becoming a victim, *if* you've correctly identified the top 20% of habits that could have made you vulnerable to crime or accident exposure. Whilst this is not an exact science, I trust you get the idea.

In terms of target hardening, we once again have to really take-on the perspective of the attacker, criminal or terrorist and understand what it is that we could do personally to make our workplace, our homes and our family an unattractive target, or ensure that we are not simply caught at the wrong time and the wrong place, when something negative happens. Referring back to earlier principles in this book, it is critical to find a balance. Paranoia is as negative as not being aware at all. The goal of this book is to truly enhance your quality of life through elimination of fear and minimization of stress related to not knowing how to handle situations and to help keep you and your family safe and to not drive unnecessary expenditure of energy worrying about all the possible things that could go wrong.

To achieve this, we need to be able to understand how criminals pick targets. As discussed in the last section, there is obviously a basis of a risk vs reward decision modelling which may account for the majority of criminal attacks. To counter a basic risk vs reward targeting model, we simply need not advertise the fact that we have things that Wolves may want, i.e. if I'm walking down the road wearing lots of gold jewelry – even if I'm in a so-called safe area – I may attract unwanted attention. This is not to tell you how you have to behave but to make you aware of the consequences that such behavior may cause.

We have trained thousands of women in our personal safety, self-defense and rape prevention courses. Very often we'll get a lady who will say something like "it's not fair. It's not right. I should be able to wear whatever I want and conduct myself however I want." Whilst ideologically we agree that, in reality this may not be so, from a personal safety perspective, that sort of attitude may lead to unwanted attention and unwanted problems. Whether we like it or not, the norms of moral rights, human rights, freedom of movement and freedom of expression are not always the norms of attackers, terrorists and criminals.

When it comes down to assessing how to target harden ourselves, the starting point is to try and eliminate the access to what the potential opposition may want. This is not always possible so the next aspect is that if we can eliminate what it is they want, then make sure that it's hard for them to get it. We don't have to make it impossible. All we have to do is make it harder for them to get what they want from us than it is from others, so that they pick another target. While it's not necessarily fair to say rather rob, steal, rape, assault or hurt another person instead of you, at the end of the day, until each person takes responsibility for their own personal safety, this is about all we can do.

Building on the base of actions and activities we can apply to make ourselves hard targets, let's start off with the concept of 'defense in depth.' 'Defense in depth' is a security concept that has also been applied in many other contexts. It's also often called the 'onion ring approach' and sometimes referred to as 'concentric layers' or 'circles.' The idea is quite simply based on the premise that it's not about applying one method or one approach that makes you a hard target, but applying as many layers as possible, i.e. the more layers you have the more you will be viewed as an unattractive target (refer to chapter 1 – section on Risk management for a diagram of defense in depth).

IN TERMS OF DEFENSE-IN-DEPTH, LET'S START WITH YOUR HOME, AND WORK FROM THE OUTSIDE IN…

In determining layers, let's start off looking at something basic like your house. Depending on where you live, you may not need any layers. That's where your base lining and general threat assessment understanding is important – particularly from a quality of life perspective. To set yourself up as though your house is a jail in an environment where this is not required, is firstly an unnecessary expense and finally may even have the opposite effect because criminals or people targeting you may perceive that there must be something valuable based on the level of protection that you've put in place.

In terms of a 'Defense in Depth' approach in a residential security context, let's start from the outside and understand that by selecting a geographic area first based on safety and crime, then looking down to the next level being the street you live in and your neighbors. From there, looking at the borders of your house. Is there a fence? Is there a need for a fence? Look at whether you need CCTV, dogs, cameras or lights on the outside of the house. Assess what sort of gate or door you need. Make sure that there's protection on the windows. Do you need a burglar alarm or some sort of early warning system? In extreme circumstances, would you need additional internal barriers, such as a gate to separate off the living area from the sleeping area or even a safe room or holding area?

Considering all of the aspects mentioned above, the reality is that what would make your house unattractive is not necessarily any one of these measures specifically, but the sum total of all these different tools being applied in a 'defense in-depth' or 'layered' approach. Whilst in many cases you may want to engage a security expert to advise on these issues, it is not always necessary as a logical approach may be enough in many cases.

If we took you as an individual, walking down the street and we looked at what could be done to make you a hard or unattractive target, it would primarily start with a base level of awareness. In most cases criminals and attackers would pick people who wouldn't see them coming, seem distracted or seem unaware. Based on this simple concept, small actions such as being extra careful when we talk on our mobile phones, when we listen to music or when we're totally distracted should be worth considering if the area and people there posed a risk or perhaps was unfamiliar or even unknown. It's not to say we should never do these things, but we should do them in an environment where the potential of attack is very slim. Therefore, our ability to switch from color yellow to color white is valid and would be considered safe.

FALSE CONFIDENCE IS PERCEPTION BASED, WHEREAS REAL CONFIDENCE IS BASED ON ABILITIES AND HAVING A PLAN.

Whilst understanding the need to become a hard or unpalatable target is comparatively straight forward, the starting point to applying this personal target hardening or personal 'defense in depth' approach is truly as simple as base level awareness. It's important that we are not only aware of what's going on around us, but that potential attackers see us being aware through actions such as us looking around and observing and controlling our personal space. It doesn't help if <u>we</u> know we're aware, but nobody else can <u>see</u> that we're aware. Visibly turning your head and scanning your environment is a very useful tool. Utilizing observational aids around you, like glass windows in storefront shops, which may provide reflection or mirrors, which will enable you to see behind you, provide an additional level of awareness and observation.

It is true that if you pick up almost any book or manual on personal safety or self-defense, one of the critical ingredients almost guaranteed to be mentioned is that if you don't want to be a victim or a target, you shouldn't act like one – that confidence is, in itself, a massive deterrent. That may be true, but we need to be very careful to ensure that we have real confidence and not false confidence. False confidence is perception based, whereas real confidence is based on abilities and having a plan.

Let's consider a good example, *imagine, you are walking down the road and two suspicious men are following you. You've mapped your route and you know that there's a safe haven, such as a police station or hospital area roughly a 100 meters ahead but you note that just to the left, there are some suspicious men about 100–150 meters away. You should be able to exhibit a high level of confidence because you know that before they could get to you and harm you, you'd be able to reach your safe haven.* Building on the concept of real vs. perceived confidence, let's say you're in good physical shape and you're used to running and you may have confidence that if you have to break into a sprint or run, the likelihood of you being able to outrun the suspicious men before they could harm you creates a very real level of confidence. Having said that, if you don't have the confidence in many cases it is better to fake it then be perceived to be vulnerable and an 'easy victim'.

Over and above being aware, controlling your personal space and carrying yourself with confidence, another layer may be that you've undertaken some form of self-defense or personal safety training. The confidence of knowing that if you had to fight and protect yourself or others, you're able to, provides another significant layer. Building on this concept, depending on where you live, you may be able to carry tools, such as pepper sprays or other self-protection aids. While we should never become dependent on these tools, because when we remove them we ultimately lose our confidence if it's based on having the said tool, carrying, and knowing how to use such tools, becomes another layer to provide you with an additional level of confidence.

While we want to ensure that our confidence is based on a real capability and a real plan, from a potential attacker's perspective, they don't know whether your confidence is based on you having a plan and being able to defend yourself or whether you're just faking it. In the absence of self-defense skills and having a solid plan, the old saying of 'fake it until you make it' most definitely applies. If you can ensure that people perceive you to be confident, that you know where you are, you know what you're doing, it will be unclear from your oppositions perspective whether its real or fake so it becomes a great strategy towards making you a hard target.

In summary, in terms of personal safety and making yourself an unattractive target here is a quick list of useful actions to apply when on foot:

- Always try and make sure you are familiar with your route.
- Identify likely areas of risk.
- Identify safe havens (any place with lots of light and lots of people).
- Match your level of awareness (color codes) to what is happening around you.
- Be careful of getting distracted by things such as talking on your phone in unknown areas or places where you may be vulnerable.
- Scan and observe and make sure you actually turn your head.
- Use items such as mirrors or glass to increase your observational capability.
- When possible, walk in groups.
- Don't display items of value and secure bags, wallets etc. to your person.
- Carry yourself with confidence but if you can't, 'fake it till you make it'.
- Ideally learn some basic self-defense.
- Scan your environment for defensive tools.

- If you are allowed to, and the risk level is real, carrying legal self-defense aids such as a pepper spray is a useful option.
- Don't exhibit signs of being scared or nervous – this makes you look like an easy target.

(please see Annexure for more scenario based examples and guidelines)

Putting it altogether

In summarizing this concept, we can refer back to the 'COI triangle'. C stands for capability. O stands for opportunity. I stands for intent. Triangles require all three sides for structural integrity. Remove one side of the triangle and the triangular structure collapses. When we look at capability, opportunity and intent, we truly can't control criminal or terrorist capability. As discussed previously when we talked about aspects such as technology, self-radicalization, the comparatively easy access to weaponry or the access to learning know-how – never before has it been easier for our opposition to gain the skills that they require to combat attacks or cause harm. Therefore, from our perspective, we need to make sure that we focus on removing the opportunity.

Intent is something that we can't control either. While many governments are launching programs to counter violent extremism and violence reduction activities, the truth of the matter is these are comparatively long-term approaches and it's going to be very hard to measure tangible results in the short to medium term. While we should most definitely focus on root causes, and on a high level, try and mitigate the starting points for such activities, the fact is, on a global basis, violence and violent behavior are probably not going to be going anywhere any time soon, therefore, we cannot really do much about intent.

The primary objective, when it comes to assessing the likelihood and the consequence of somebody targeting you in different situations, needs to lean very much towards proactivity. Our opposition has all the time to think up different methods of attack. Our starting point, therefore, is to remember that attackers will always conduct some sort of pre-attack surveillance or pre-attack victim selection – often referred to as an attacker ritual. If during this phase we are able to present ourselves as a hard target, it's quite likely we won't be selected or the attacker, of their own accord, may decide to abort the attack based on it being too hard and possibly not providing an easy opportunity for success. In other words, their risk vs reward equation hasn't quite matched up.

We need to apply all of these tools when we look at assessing threat, risk and hazard levels. Unfortunately, based on us not knowing the mental state of an attacker, we need to look at worst case scenarios and we need to be realistic about what we can and can't do. We need to drive our effort in making sure we prevent or avoid situations as our primary, or 80% energy, focus area. Therefore, it comes down to how much we are willing to do in advance, and how habitually we are able to integrate safety and security into the way we behave in the physical world and online.

Finally, we come to the last concept in terms of assessing potential issues and trying to make sure that we don't misdiagnose threat and risk levels based on paranoia or inaccurate intuitive response. You might clinically analyze a situation. You might look at the likelihood and the consequence. When trying to proactively assess threat and risk, you might look at all the different variables that may occur and come up blank, but for some reason your intuition may tell you that there's still an issue or there's still a problem. When this happens, generally speaking, we revert back to our initial focus of 'if there is doubt, there is no doubt'. If your intuition has been triggered, it's probably been triggered for a reason. When we look at what that reason may be in an after action analysis, we very often realize, once again, that our intuition provided relevant early warning cues. As such, when it comes to the safety of you and your loved ones – when in doubt, even if you can't consciously assess and determine the likelihood and consequence of an event, but your intuition flags – you should trust it implicitly and rather take the route of caution because even if it's wrong – it's better to be safe than sorry...

Chapter summary

The goal of making yourself a hard target is basically designed to provide criminals with the feedback that after assessing you, compared to other options, you are an unpalatable target as you do not present as an easy victim. The primary principle behind this is that in most cases, criminals will run a basic risk vs. reward equation when evaluating and selecting a potential target, even if this is a very quick process. If it does not look like you have what they're after – or if it's not so easy to actually determine if there is an accessible reward there or if you don't have easily accessible items and even from a rapist's perspective, if you never provided any opportunity for them to get close to you, it's very difficult for them to target you and as such they will probably look for an easier target. When we really look at the core of what we need to do, it is useful to remember that most of the time, criminals will take the path of least resistance. If we strive to make ourselves a difficult target, they are unlikely to select us and will simply seek to choose an easier target.

Once you are confident you can apply the skills of your awareness toolbox and understand the basics of attacker ritual and target hardening, centered around removing the opportunity for an attacker to target you, the last issue to become familiar with is the reactive requirements and capabilities you should have if an incident actually occurred. This focuses on your ability to respond, if necessary, and deal with dangerous situations. We'll talk about that in the next chapter when we focus on taking action to try and ensure that you can physically avoid or intervene and manage a situation, by applying the run, hide, fight and communicate approach.

CHAPTER 5

Taking Action

Introduction to strategic and tactical response

The ability to act effectively truly comes down to the amount of preparation we put in however, we are all wired slightly differently and have to contend with what is sometimes referred to as the neural seesaw. As described by Matthew D. Lieberman, PhD in his excellent book " Social: Why Our Brains Are Wired to Connect"[1]:

> *"Our brains have made it difficult to be both socially and analytically focused at the same time. Even though thinking social and analytically don't feel radically different, evolution built our brain with different networks for handling these two ways of thinking. In the frontal lobe, regions on the outer surface, closer to the skull, are responsible for analytical thinking and are highly related to IQ. In contrast, regions in the middle of the brain, where the two hemispheres touch, support social thinking. These regions allow us to piece together a person's thoughts, feelings, and goals based on what we see from their actions, words, and context. Here's the really surprising thing about the brain. These two networks function like a neural seesaw".*

---

[1] *For more information see: Lieberman, M. D. (2013). Social: Why our brains are wired to connect. New York, NY: Crown.*

In other words, it's really hard to be analytical and emotive at the same time. It is equally hard to be responding to an issue with an instinctive response and thinking rationally at the same time – in fact, it's almost impossible without effective Adrenal Response Management, which requires the combination of strategic capability and the ability to perform under pressure (tactical capability). A personal challenge is to grow both skill sets so that you are able to be both strategic and tactical in your thinking (and even in your actions) as different situations dictate. This is summarized in the graphic below:

STRATEGIC
You have time
Make sure you identify and prioritise effectively
Apply formal risk based standards and guidelines
Be thorough and think it through
Ensure Stakeholder consultation
Have a plan A, B and C
Integrate solutions
Red team solutions
Modify and update solutions

TACTICAL
No time
Gut instinct, based on intuitive programming
Adrenal dump = Necessity for adrenal response management
If you have not planned response is down to luck and experience
OODA LOOP/Situational awareness
Failing to plan is planning to fail...

The focus of this chapter will align more with the Tactical aspects but it should be constantly taken into consideration that strategic planning and preparation is critical to ensure we are actually able to perform under stress.

Run, hide, fight, communicate and adrenalin

The starting point for being able to make sure that you act in an appropriate manner when faced with an intense situation – whether it be to remain cool, calm and collected or trigger your internal aggression switch, is understanding that the more prepared you are, the more capable you are of performing reasonably well under extreme stress. The way we respond to any situation, the way we manage our instinctive adrenal responses – often referred to as the flight or fight instinct – is the critical starting point. It doesn't help to come up with a complex plan as to where you would run, where you would hide or in an extreme circumstance, how you would fight, if you're not able to control yourself and you land up freezing and/ or panicking at a critical time where reaction and response are required.

To truly understand adrenalin, we need to understand the pros and cons of our adrenal response as well as the management and coping mechanisms associated with the way our adrenal response actually works. The term 'stress inoculation' is very often used when it comes to preparing people to react under intense crisis-type situations. Despite the proven effectiveness of stress inoculation to prepare people for complex situations, the truth is that most normal, everyday people generally don't have the time or resources to properly undergo effective stress inoculation training, relating in particular to having to run, hide or fight from something life threatening. If you just think of a worst-case scenario – let's take an active shooter situation where, to role play a live active shooter scenario and ensure that you are able to perform effectively under stress, is a massive undertaking. To ensure that it's done safely both from a physical as well as a psychological point of view is a whole issue in itself. The sheer coordination of this often means that it's something that most people will not be exposed to. When it comes to lower level threats and more likely incidents such as personal assault or even managing a fire or medical emergency, we need to have skills to manage situations such as these examples even if we can't participate in a large-scale stress inoculation activity.

When it comes to looking at the way we stress inoculate and how we develop the capability to respond, we have to be very pragmatic. As previously mentioned – the starting point is understanding how our fight and flight and adrenal response actually work. The reality is that the fight or flight response has kept our species alive for thousands and thousands of years, so it clearly has some major benefits. However, we need to take into account the fact that originally the fight or flight instinct was primarily designed to keep us safe from predators or animals that were bigger and meaner than us – not necessarily the modern day complex threat issues we face such as Cyber Threats. As an example of how our instinctive response was developed –

Imagine you were walking through the forest several thousand years ago, minding your own business, picking berries and having a pretty good time. All of a sudden, out of the blue, this giant sabre tooth tiger jumps out in front of you. Without even thinking at all, your instinct is initially going to be to run away and the overwhelming flight response will be the primary driver. In fact, you would only turn and fight with this much bigger, stronger, more aggressive animal if you had absolutely no other choice and could not potentially run away and escape or if you had to engage to protect a loved one.

This evolutionary instinctive response has stayed with our species to this day, where the majority of us are actually flight dominant. There is a small minority who tend to be wired slightly differently and often exhibit sociopathic or psychopathic tendencies whereby their tendency to lean towards the fight instead of flight as a first response is stronger. This doesn't always mean that people like that would be criminals or predators. Many of them often become our bravest Sheepdogs choosing vocations such as becoming special forces soldiers or specialist police officers based on their ability to instinctively perform at a critical output by confronting danger instead of running away from it.

Having said that, because the vast majority (estimates are as high as 98%) of the population is flight dominant, we need firstly understand

THE CORE CONCERN TENDS TO HINGE AROUND THE SIDE EFFECTS THAT CAN OFTEN ACCOMPANY AN INTENSE ADRENAL RESPONSE – THE ISSUES OF FREEZING OR PANICKING.

how to manage this response in an effective way. In addition, the old saying that "it's better to run away and live to fight another day" has a lot of wisdom to it, especially when dealing with an attack situation you may not have been ready for. Fleeing or fighting, in essence, is not a good or bad thing. It just hinges around the timing of when you do which and whether the fight or the flight is the appropriate response for the particular scenario. Furthermore, the core concept of concern is not so much around fight or flight, because if you're fighting or fleeing, it means you're actually doing something. The core concern tends to hinge around the side effects that can often accompany an intense adrenal response – the issues of freezing or panicking.

Freezing or panicking at the wrong time may have extreme consequences. If you freeze when you're behind the wheel of a car and you need to slam on the brakes or change lanes, or if you panic in the same situation, it literally may cost lives. Whenever we're talking about adrenal response management (A.R.M), we often tend to focus on the worst-case scenarios, however the ability to apply A.R.M translates itself directly to everyday life and situational management, dealing with the stresses and pressures of modern living as much as it does to life or death decision making.

To gain true insight, we need to divide adrenal response into two broad categories. Firstly, we have positive things that happen to help us and secondly, we have negative things happen which may hinder our performance. Generally speaking, positive things are enablers. Things such as the fact that we become stronger, become faster, feel less pain and become more focused on a specific objective are all positive outcomes. Conversely, negative outcomes include aspects such as tunnel vision, whereby you lose your peripheral vision and become fixated on only what is directly in front of you or what is perceived as the largest threat; auditory exclusion or distortion, whereby you don't hear at all or what you hear is distorted; verbal inability, which

WE TEND TO REMEMBER THINGS THAT WERE TRAUMATIC IN A WAY THAT IS LESS TRAUMATIC FOR US. AS SUCH, OUR RECALL OF EVENTS AND THE WAY THEY HAPPENED, IN OUR AFTER-ACTION PROCESSING, MAY NOT NECESSARILY BE ACCURATE. THEREFORE, IT MAY NOT BE AS SIMPLE AS WE THINK TO LEARN FROM INTENSE SITUTAIONS.

means that the part of your brain that controls complex speech activity, totally shuts down, so your ability to communicate effectively is almost nil.

There can also be time, space and memory distortion. Time either speeds up or slows down, but your perception of time is not necessarily accurate. Space refers to distance. The ability to tell how far away things are often becomes quite a tough task under an adrenal dump. When we talk about memory, there are usually two critical outputs. One is that you are unlikely to be able to apply what is not instinctive or reflexive under an adrenal dump or an intensive injection of adrenalin into your system. This means if we want to be sure that we could respond effectively under critical situations, we would most likely need a significant amount of training and experience to improve our odds of performing effectively.

Secondly, we tend to remember things that were traumatic in a way that is less traumatic for us. As such, our recall of events and the way they happened, in our after-action processing, may not necessarily be accurate. As an example – *it is for that exact reason, that police detectives need to seek out as many witnesses as possible after a crime because everyone remembers traumatic situations in a slightly different way or blocks out certain realities and aspects when recalling what happened.*

From a performance perspective, a normal resting heart rate may be between 60 and 80 beats per minute. Once you get an adrenal dump (a huge injection of adrenalin based on exposure to an immediately threatening event), your heart rate shoots up to roughly 150–200 beats a minute. It's important to understand this quick acceleration to action. In sporting psychology, there's a concept referred to as the 'inverted U hypothesis'. The 'inverted U hypothesis' highlights the issues of how over and under stimulation can affect performance. In simplistic terms, if you're under-stimulated, in other words your heart rates may possibly be under 100 beats a minute, you're probably not going to perform optimally. This is primarily because the positive adrenal response factors such as speed, strength and focus may not be engaged. Conversely, if you're hyper-stimulated, where your heart rate might be above

150 beats a minute, you also will not perform effectively. This is because the negative signs and symptoms of adrenalin will become the primary actors. Aspects such as tunnel vision, auditory exclusion, loss of fine motor skill, etc. will take precedence and limit performance. As such, one of the goals and objectives is to find the right level of stimulation – roughly between 100 and 145 beats per minute, which would enable you to perform effectively, without all the negative side effects becoming overruling factors but having the benefits of the positive ones. It sounds very simple, but unfortunately, it's not so easy to actually achieve.

Adrenalin also has many other factors that come in to play, for example in extreme situations, you may wet yourself, defecate or throw up because when it comes to running or fighting, a full bladder, full intestines and your digestive system being active are not critical to immediate survival in that given moment. Simply put – you can run faster with empty bowels and bladder.

ADRENAL RESPONSE DRAMATICALLY HINDERS FINE MOTOR SKILL BUT ENHANCES GROSS MOTOR MOVEMENTS!

Now most of us experience some level of adrenal response or activation almost every day when we encounter stressful issues such as getting into an argument or getting cut off in traffic. The adrenal response we experience almost daily is intricately connected to our fighting or fleeing survival responses. However, because we very rarely land up fighting or fleeing, we may experience attributable symptoms such as butterflies in the stomach, cold shivers, cold sweats, shaking or nervous twitching because our larger muscle fill with blood and our digestive system and non-critical survival brain functions shut down to make us faster and stronger.

In addition, there are also other side effects such as the loss of fine motor skills, whereby we lose our ability to perform small and precise movements. Activities such as dialing a phone number, sticking your finger in somebody's eye in a life or death self-defense situation, or even putting a key into a lock all become difficult to perform under intense adrenal dump. Conversely, gross motor skill capability increases.

The ability to perform large movements become more effective. By understanding this, you can better plan for the way you are likely to react and perform under intense pressure.

Coupled with all of these signs and symptoms of adrenalin is an instinctive response called the 'flinch response'. The 'flinch response' is an instinctive response to a threat or something that takes us by surprise. It usually consists of three primary movements or aspects:

- A sharp inhalation;
- Pulling the limbs into the body;
- Moving away from the threat.

Now this is an instinctive response that has helped keep our species alive for thousands of years, but when it comes to running, hiding or fighting, it may not necessarily be the most effective response in terms of modern day threats and challenges. As an example – *we know for a fact that in the majority of cases, when it comes to responding to a violent attack and defending yourself, moving back only creates a stronger psychological advantage for your attacker, but, because it is instinctive, we need to be aware of it so we can try and manage and mitigate it.*

In our training sessions, we have seen the negative issues of adrenal and flinch responses overwhelm participants hundreds of times. We have even had people faint when participating in live reality based scenarios because under adrenal response, they forgot to breathe when their flinch response kicked in. This may sound strange because obviously we're all experts in breathing since we do it all day, every day, but the way we respond under intense stress is a slightly different reality.

When we start to assess all of these variables, we need to look at adrenal response from three perspectives.

1. **How does it affect you as an individual?**
   Our instinctive response, whilst very similar, are all a bit different because we are all wired and have evolved slightly differently.

Some people experience tremendous tunnel vision and auditory exclusion, while others have almost none. Other people are prone to panic whilst some people can stay cool and calm under pressure. This is why practical training is one of the most important undertakings for preparing us to perform effectively under stress. Unfortunately, it is also one of the most expensive, time-consuming and dangerous parts of prepping ourselves when we want to stress inoculate. When it comes to looking at the way we manage adrenal response for ourselves, we also need to understand that we all have limited time, effort and energy in the way we would prepare to manage adrenal response. In addition, your individual sleep cycles, personality, emotional and physical state will have a significant impact on the way you respond. The primary reason we look at this from the perspective of 'you' as the first consideration is that if you can't effectively manage your own fight or flight instinct to the point that you don't freeze and don't panic, your ability to actually survive a critical situation may be severely impinged.

2. **The second perspective is to look at what would be happening to your attacker.**

The attacker would also experience intense adrenal dump. While you may be calm enough, for example, to talk to them and explain to them why they shouldn't hurt you, because of their own adrenal dump, they may not be hearing whatever you're trying to say as a result of their own auditory exclusion. They may also lose fine motor skills. In fact, as an example – *it's been both scary and interesting to find that sometimes there are very negative outcomes attributed to loss of fine motor skill and the flinch response from an attacker perspective. Over the years we have run thousands of armed robbery and vehicle hijacking simulations, where we utilize training guns and we let our role-player participants commit the crimes on each other to assess the way that individuals react and perform. In roughly 50% of these situations, we found that our participants unintentionally pulled the trigger of the training gun.* This presents a scary finding and a harsh reality because the flinch response is so strong that even just a small movement by the victim that was unexpected from the attackers' perspective could result in a flinch. When handling a firearm, this flinch response usually means that somebody may pull the trigger unintentionally. Understanding the way adrenalin affects the potential attackers or assailants is a critical step in terms of planning how to respond from a run, hide, fight perspective.

3. **Lastly, we need to look at the way adrenal response would affect other people in an extreme situation**.

    We need to understand adrenal response effectively from this perspective in terms of you adopting a sheepdog role. If you were the one who had to manage an evacuation or coordinate people under crisis, the ability to communicate and the ability for them to understand or respond is dramatically affected by adrenal response. Clear and rational thinking and the ability to perform may be seriously affected in those around you. You need to factor in these issues, as in many cases, you may be responsible for your family members or other people based on your ability to respond, and the fact that you have actually put some effort into preparation. If we don't understand this, the ability to effectively act in support of others and make sure people function correctly to save their own lives, may be severely impinged.

What this boils down to, is that we need to look at the way we can manage and overcome freeze and panic to ensure that if we have to, we can respond under pressure. The fight and flight response used correctly are valuable survival tools. So the core question is:

How do we ensure we don't freeze and panic? – We need to master A.R.M

The correct methodology to apply Adrenal Response Management (A.R.M) incorporates four key aspects that will be discussed in some depth.

> WE NEED TO LOOK AT THE WAY WE CAN MANAGE AND OVERCOME FREEZE AND PANIC TO ENSURE THAT IF WE HAVE TO, WE CAN RESPOND UNDER PRESSURE.

ARM Tool 1: Realistic, repetitive, effective training and experience

The first key aspect is the aspect of realistic, repetitive, effective training and experience. We tend to fear most what we don't understand. As an example – *If you think back to the first time you drove a car, this might have been traumatic for you. In all likelihood, it was probably more traumatic for the person teaching you. However, if you're now an experienced driver, you've probably done this activity thousands and thousands of times to the point where it's an instinctive and reflexive skill. The thought of doing this no longer scares you or intimidates you in any way, shape or form.* This example is directly transferable to learning to conduct any complex activity which may include life or death decisions and split-second response capability.

In terms of being able to perform effectively under the most extreme situations such as an encountering a violent armed robber, facing an active shooter, surviving a terrorist incident, or even just performing CPR on someone – the ability to undergo realistic, repetitive, effective training is a very difficult ask for the average person. In fact, to safely gain experience and context with sufficient repetitions to acclimatize, is realistically an impossibility for most people due to limitations in time, access and resources. One of the other issues in responding effectively to worst case situations is that unfortunately, most of the time, we are primed to the way these events happen by what we see on TV and in the movies. As previously discussed the way things are portrayed is not always an accurate reflection of the way things actually happen. That's why, despite the complexities, I would strongly urge everyone to undertake, at the very least, some training to build confidence around the way one may react in these critical incidents. This could be a basic self-defense course or making sure that your first aid is current.

Since it is expensive, dangerous and difficult to conduct reality style training to gain the experience you need in a wide range of worst case scenarios, and because of the core principle that we would not like to expose ourselves to additional danger unless absolutely necessary, we definitely don't want to try an event simulation unless its run by professionals and supervised in a safe manner. As an example of a poor preparatory idea – *imagine, you pick a dangerous neighborhood in your city, you take some money and you put it in your top pocket so that it's exposed. You go for a walk with the 'aim of being robbed' so you can learn to manage the situation. You get robbed and the first time you panic. The next time you're calmer. If you're lucky enough to survive to the third or fourth event, well you may even then have mastered your own freeze or panic response.* However, the dangers of that sort of planning and behavior are obviously way too high and the risk doesn't warrant the benefit. So we should be very critical of the way we gain the ability to stay cool, calm and collected in worst case scenarios. I urge you to evaluate potential training options based on the 5 Principles of real world violence previously discussed and ensure that if you do undertake training, that it is training that prepares you effectively and is not a waste of your time. Because of the limitations mentioned ARM tool 2 is very important for us to bridge the gaps…

ARM tool 2: Visualization and mental role play

My sincere wish is that, if you are honest with yourself and find that whilst reading this book has been a big step forward, you may be one of those people who is unlikely to undertake any practical training in which case, the concept of realistic, repetitive, effective training and experience is just not a viable option for you and you would just be misleading yourself if you thought it would be… However, you need not worry as we have a shortcut for you – ARM Tool 2: the application of visualization and mental role play. Whilst it is not a substitute for realistic, repetitive, effective training and experience, it is certainly a very useful bridge towards helping you prepare and enhance the likelihood of effective performance under pressure. Obviously, the combination of visualization and mental role play (ARM tool 2) with realistic, repetitive, effective training and experience (ARM Tool 1) would yield better results than on its own, but it is certainly better than doing nothing.

Once you know how to utilize the tools of visualization and mental role-play, they become extremely valuable in preparing you to respond effectively in worst case scenarios. There's been extensive research conducted regarding the way that people perform under stress. Specifically, in the fields of sports psychology, decision making and performance, there have been many research projects that look at sportsmen and women and the way they rehearse, practice and prepare to perform under extreme stress and pressure. Universally, these studies have all found that utilizing visualization and mental role play both improve performance in a very real and tangible way. Using these tools is also a great 'cheat' from a time commitment perspective because if you're only willing to allocate, say five or ten minutes a week, to your personal safety and worst-case scenario planning, then the only option you have is realistic visualization or mental role play to try and program your instinctive and reflexive response.

To summarize a very complex topic, there are two main ways to apply visualization and mental role play. One is referred to as 'active', where you're actually in the situation and you see your limbs moving in front of you, i.e. in the first person. It's almost as though you're playing a first person video game. The second way is referred to as 'passive', where it's almost like sitting back and watching yourself on a screen performing activities. Which technique is the more effective one really depends on you as an individual and what you find easier to do. What is important in terms of visualization or mental role play is to try and keep your visualization as realistic as possible. Research has shown that we should apply what is called the 'minimum Three Senses Rule'. Different senses are located in different parts of our brain – sight, smell, touch, hearing and taste all have different activation centers. The more senses you can involve when you visualize, the more parts of the brain are involved and stimulated, and the more real your subconscious perceives the process to be. This will result in an enhanced preparatory benefit from your activity. If you've ever had a dream from which you wake and you have to re-orientate yourself because that dream felt so real, this illustrates how real your mental role play can become.

When applying visualization or mental role play, you need to be very careful not to go off on tangents and transfer from an active activity to daydreaming. Daydreaming or visualizing unrealistic scenarios along with idealistic improbable responses has very little benefit. This is because when the time comes for you to actually respond, you would not have programmed any accurate responses into your subconscious memory and therefore will have no context for response. So, in summary, it's critically important from a preparatory benefit perspective to make sure that you are firstly able to visualize realistically, secondly, be able to involve your senses in a practical and realistic way when doing this and lastly strive to keep the process realistic and minizine the 'daydreaming factor'.

> WHEN APPLYING VISUALIZATION OR MENTAL ROLE PLAY, YOU NEED TO BE VERY CAREFUL TO NOT GO OFF ON TANGENTS AND BECOME A DAYDREAMER. DAYDREAMING OR VISUALIZING UNREALISTIC SCENARIOS ALONG WITH IDEALISTIC RESPONSES HAS VERY LITTLE BENEFIT.

In making sure that you are able to perform effectively under stress and that your visualization activities actually have a benefit, you need to work hard to try and ensure that you relate to your three-point check system (3PC-S) practices and the other aspects of your Awareness Toolbox and the way you visualise. It is important to ensure that you are actually visualizing based on real and live issues as opposed to things that may just be in your imagination i.e. preparing yourself for real and not just perceived risks. Over the years I have spoken with hundreds of people who have been exposed to, or have actually been victims of criminal, terrorist, emergency or medical situations and I always try to question, those who are willing, to share as thoroughly as possible. I urge you to do the same. We often think people don't want to talk about traumatic events but I have found that when approached from a non-judgmental, lessons learned perspective, people are usually happy to share. I urge you to do the same, asking how things happened and what people could have done differently, as answers can provide very useful context for you. In addition, reflecting on past actual incidents and the way they happened, and then using both aspects as a basis for the way you visualize and conduct mental role play, can have massive benefits for you – just remember the reality of memory distortion that comes into play when traumatic events are recalled.

ARM tool 3: Breathing and Stress management

Firstly, on a practical basis, one of the critical coping mechanisms and response tools to traumatic events and every day stress is simply learning how to breathe effectively. Whilst breathing is always taught in martial arts, the concept of tactical or applied breathing has become quite a well-known tool. Under any stressful situation, simply remembering to breathe deeply and control your breathing will reduce your heart rate, re-oxygenate your system, and enhance your ability to perform effectively. This can be applied in numerous different ways but the simplest approach is referred to as tactical breathing and works as follows – breathe in for the count of four, hold your breath for the count of four, exhale for the count of four, hold your breath for another count of four and then repeat. Running this sort of cycle, programs you to be able to re-oxygenate and increase your ability to stay calm. If you are able to stay calm during a situation and move to what we described as a stimulated state, as opposed to hyper-stimulated or under-stimulated states, the ability to perform effectively is, without doubt, improved.

The second aspect of ARM tool 3 is basic stress management. Stress management is closely aligned with the final ARM tool 4, physical health and conditioning but deserves to be mentioned under this heading as well. If you are already stressed and in an emotionally unstable state, your ability to deal with a high stress situation will be negatively affected. As such, general stress management, which includes all the aspects that will be outlined in the final ARM tool 4 – physical health and conditioning – also extends to issues such as relationship management, work/life balance and attitudinal stability.

ARM tool 4: Physical Health and Conditioning

The last ARM tool is to strive to maintain a decent level of physical health and conditioning. Aside from managing the direct threats associated with bad health so the that you can live longer and be more active, the effects of intense adrenal dump are very similar to those of intense physical exercise. You don't necessarily have to be a triathlete but if you are in shape, your muscles are used to filling with blood, your heart rate is used to shooting up suddenly and therefore your ability to respond in high stress activities when facing an adrenal dump, should be improved because it's less traumatic for your body and a familiar experience for you. The basics of healthy eating, regular effective exercise cannot be underrated. It does not help that you are prepared for every worse case scenario you can think of but ignore the obvious reality that disease is our biggest threat and risk therefore staying healthy is a critical life activity.

ARM in summary

Now that we have an understanding of the basics of the critical aspects of adrenal response and adrenal response management, we can move on to the next level, which involves focusing on what we should actually do when we are faced with worst case scenarios.

However, before we move on, let's just double check that you are now comfortable with where we are so far. The basics of understanding adrenal response are important from three perspectives:

1. Understanding and managing your own adrenal and stress responses
2. Understanding and working around your attacker's adrenal and stress responses

3. **Understanding and managing other people's adrenal and stress responses**

In order to perform, we need to apply the 4 tools of Adrenal Response Management (A.R.M)

- **A.R.M Tool 1: Realistic, repetitive, effective training and experience**
- **A.R.M Tool 2: Visualization and mental role play**
- **A.R.M Tool 3: Breathing and Stress management**
- **A.R.M Tool 4: Physical Health and Conditioning**

We have covered the concept of using realistic training and experience to build a platform from which to be able to visualize. On a practical basis, being able to remember tactical breathing and applying it is also a great help under stress. We need to strive for healthy living and to stay in shape so that we are physically resilient and able to cope with challenges as they manifest.

Non-physical and physical aggression

It is important to take note of the fundamental differences between physical and non-physical aggression. In essence, if someone is demonstrating non-physical aggression whereby they may be threatening you verbally or showing aggressive body language with threatening gestures and you can't escape or avoid the situation, your goal is to as soon as possible determine if you can de-escalate the situation or not. Whilst maintaining a safe separation (i.e. a gap whereby people can't physically touch you) and your hands are up forming a protective barrier with your hands between you and the aggressor. The goal is to try and engage the aggressors thinking brain (System 2) so that the more primal instincts governed by the animal brain (System 1) can be brought under control. There are several ways to achieve this but one of the key ways to do it is to ask disengaging open ended questions that require consideration, i.e. please tell me why you are so angry? or how can I help you to resolve the issue that has frustrated you? This needs to accompany many other key variables which include the following:

- ✓ Maintaining a non-threatening but protective body position
- ✓ Maintaining a safe separation and space
- ✓ Maintaining a calm tone of voice
- ✓ Using effective nonverbal communication
- ✓ Trying to build rapport – the sooner you can get the aggressors name and talk to them using their name the better
- ✓ Showing empathy and trying to get the aggressor to simply say the word "yes" or "ok"
- ✓ Active listening is critical but should not distract from assessing whether the incident will transition to physical aggression.

Whilst applying disengagement and de-escalation strategies constant awareness of three key variables is critical, to determine whether the aggressor may transition to physical violence or not, these are:

- Is the aggressor moving forwards and pushing you back.
- How badly affected by adrenal response indicators is the aggressor.
- Is the aggressor trying to move your hands out of the way and constantly making physical contact.

If these three variables are happening, chances are the attack is already past the point of de-escalation and will require some level of physical protective response on your part. If the aggressor is not moving forwards or making physical contact then the issue is one of your own mental resilience and learning to control your own emotive responses, so that you are able to de-escalate such situations. This ability may sound simple but requires much practice and scenario role playing to master.

Taking action – preparing to ACT and perform

In determining the way that we're actually able to respond and take action, the core driving points comes down to a few variables – our situational awareness and our own capabilities, which then get superimposed with what is actually happening, the nature of the attack and the required response. These are all pretty complex variables to have to determine under intense stress. The solution starts once we can control our adrenal response, can figure out what are we going to do, in terms of making sure we can hopefully do the right thing at the right time. It is also critical to remember that we may not have any time at all to analyze all the variables and make decisions as such the more forethought and planning we can apply before hand the more likely we are to respond the correct way.

> WE MAY NOT HAVE ANY TIME AT ALL TO ANALYZE ALL THE VARIABLES AND MAKE DECISIONS. AS SUCH THE MORE FORETHOUGHT AND PLANNING WE CAN APPLY BEFORE HAND, THE MORE LIKELY WE ARE TO RESPOND THE CORRECT WAY.

From a practical decision-making perspective, when we look at what our different options are, a systematic approach is very useful. A very useful approach is to apply what's referred to as the 'OODA[2] loop'. The 'OODA loop' was originally developed by Col. John Boyd, a fighter pilot, to try to help fighter pilots win in air-to-air combat. The first O stands for observation. The next O stands for orientation, then comes D for decision and lastly A for action. The premise is that whoever can move through these four items faster, will likely be able to perform more effectively and survive or win the situation.

---

[2]For more information please see *Boyd, John Richard (September 3, 1976), Destruction and Creation, US Army Command and General Staff College.*

OODA Loop:

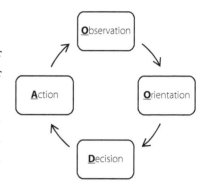

- Observation: the collection of all relevant data by means of the senses
- Orientation: the analysis and synthesis of data to form and inform one's current mental perspective
- Decision: the determination of a course of action based on one's current mental perspective and the available options
- Action: the physical playing-out of decisions

When it comes to observation, we have discussed this aspect in much detail when we looked at awareness and the awareness toolbox. When it comes to orientation, we covered this aspect as well in the chapter on assessment. When looking at decision making, we also introduced various aspects in the chapter on assessment. The previous section of this chapter that explained ARM, serves as a binding thread through the entire OODA loop process simply because if you freeze or panic, you won't be able to perform at all. When we look at taking action, we have to look at what are our options are. Whilst, it is impossible to be able to generically discuss every possible action or option, for simplicity sake we will focus on discussing the well accepted run, hide, fight (RHF) methodology in a slightly modified form that also includes the critical aspect of communication which we will refer to as the RHFC model as per the diagram alongside:

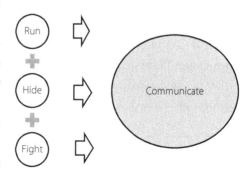

Whilst our focus should always be on proactive incident avoidance and prevention, by assessing the RHFC model, we should be able to at least come up with worst case scenario action plans. In terms of a basic stepping stone guideline to the RHFC Model, we will consider the following case example.

Imagine you are actively running your 3PC-S and you see somebody suspicious – exhibiting characteristics that make you worry in that they could be armed and seem nervous and twitchy. You determine you have enough time to call the police, i.e. before you run you determine you can communicate. The police actually arrive in time to arrest or stop that person from conducting any attack. That is a best case, first prize scenario. We refer to this as the Prevention stage of response. However, what if you could not call the police (Communication) because the threat was too close to avoid or prevent, then the direct application of the RHFC model becomes necessary. Our first point of strategy would be to RUN, escape, and if that was not possible at least HIDE. Whilst being concerned for others is always admirable but being a sheepdog means protecting others, and if you get hurt or killed, you can't help anyone else. This leads us to a tough conclusion, that whilst it is not necessarily the nicest way to look at things, you can't help anyone if you are injured or dead. This means that at the end of the day, each person is responsible for their own life first, and foremost. This process is referred to as DEFLECTION, i.e. all you can do is deflect the attack onto someone else who is a softer target than you are, especially when you are not in a position to avoid or prevent the attack.

The next level of response is based on the Running and/or Hiding Strategies not working and us therefore facing the reality of an attack. Even in this extreme situation, we would like to focus on taking a proactive approach within our own and the situational limitations. This stage is referred to as the INTERCEPT phase. This is where the attack is about to happen but you have seen it in time to recognize it, but running, hiding or calling for help is not an option. If you were going to fight, this is the most effective time to do it. By trying to take the initiative and preemptively attacking the attacker, your chances of survival improve dramatically. However, there is no doubt that there are numerous legal and consequential impact factors that need to be taken into account, i.e. if I decide to fight, I need to be totally sure that this was the right option and other preventative or avoidance options were not available.

Lastly, we look at an actual conflict or situation occurring where you have been unable to run, hide or intercept. In cases when we have not been able to apply our RHFC response, we also have available an additional response-depending on the scenario and nature of the attack – that of cooperation. In certain crimes and incidents, the criminals focus may be to get something from you. For example, in an armed robbery, if the criminal wanted to kill you, they would simply have done so. If you can stay calm and give them whatever it is that they're after, your likelihood of getting out of that situation alive and hopefully intact is probably good. Resorting to a run, hide or fight methodology once you already are in a confrontation may not actually be achievable specifically because by definition, you would have been taken by surprise and not be in an empowered position. Therefore, a cooperative approach may be the only option left. Despite this, even when adopting a strategy of cooperation, we should keep primed that we should run or may have to fight at any time. This could happen because things are so dynamic in an incident, that the 'right' strategy will most likely need to change or adapt according to hundreds of variables that may occur in a confrontation.

IN TERMS OF RESPONSE STRATEGIES TO SUPPORT THE RHFC APPROACH WE LOOK AT 4 SEQUENTIAL OPTIONS:
• PREVENT AND AVOID
• DEFLECT
• INTERCEPT
• COOPERATE

Let us now unpack each of the RHFC and the Avoid, Deflect, Intercept and Cooperate approaches and talk about them in a practical structure. In terms of running – which would hopefully be our first option – understanding where to run to and hopefully running early enough to escape, would be a great response, factoring in the need to communicate to others and the authorities so that they can hopefully intercede as soon as possible. If you were in an open area and people were shooting at you, running in a zigzag fashion, particularly if you can move from one point of cover to another can be very effective. If you are not able to effectively run, you may be stuck in terms of having to hide or fight.

When it comes to hiding, we have to understand the clear distinction between concealment – which basically provides me with protection from sight i.e. people can't see me so hopefully they can't hurt me – and cover from potential fire i.e. if somebody was shooting at me, would what I am hiding behind or in protect me? When we look at cover, we need to also understand that different weapons have different capabilities for inflicting levels of damage. I may think that a tree is effective cover, but somebody with a high caliber assault type weapon may be able to just mow the tree down very quickly. I may believe that a concrete wall provides effective cover, but somebody with heavy weaponry may be able to shoot right through the wall. Understanding the basis of what is, and what isn't effective cover is a critical starting point for worst case scenario planning. Understanding how to identify cover and moving to cover is the next reality.

Leading on from this, if there was no cover around, then at least having effective concealment is a viable option as it leaves you better off than being in a position to be easily observed. In looking as to how you would actually apply this, ideally you would look to find the best available cover or if no cover was available, then the best available concealment. Cover and Concealment generally link to the process of Hiding – a core plan should then be to try and move from a hide to a run strategy even though we should remember that this option is not always possible. You should also assess whether it is safe to try and communicate and make contact with the authorities or external parties to inform them of what is going on.

In order to make sure that you could run or get away, even when you are behind cover or hiding, you would need to ensure that you have some sort of escape plan. Unfortunately, this is also not always possible. Very often, if you decide to shelter in a place or hide, you often leave yourself with no other option than to fight if you have to, as when discovered, flight may not be an option. It's critical for us to understand that if we have no other choice but to fight, the more prepared we are, the more likely we are to be able to defend ourselves effectively and survive a situation.

Obviously, learning how to fight through undertaking self-defense or martial arts related training is a great way to start. In such case, we should align our objectives with our activities. I have been involved in the martial arts and self-defense fraternity for well over three decades now and have been fortunate enough to be exposed to some of the world's very best instructors and trainers, and have had the benefits of training in numerous locations with many different masters. The problem that I have encountered on hundreds of occasions is that what your instructor can do, is not really indicative of what you may be able to do, or what you will be likely to do under pressure or stress. When we look at the way people perform in different martial arts systems, we should be critical of the way we evaluate them from a self-defense perspective, if that is your objective... Please see Chapter 2 for more information but the points below summarize the critical issues when it comes to taking Action.

> WHEN YOU LOOK AT THE WAY PEOPLE PERFORM IN DIFFERENT MARTIAL ARTS SYSTEMS, WE SHOULD BE CRITICAL OF THE WAY WE EVALUATE THEM FROM A SELF-DEFENSE PERSPECTIVE, IF THAT IS YOUR OBJECTIVE...

People train martial arts for different reasons – some for sport, some for health, some for the arts and tradition of it. When it comes to self-defense, we have to adopt a real no-nonsense approach. That real no-nonsense approach should be based on what was discussed earlier in this book in terms of the way violence actually occurs; in terms of there being no rules; there being multiple attackers; weapons being involved; most fights being close in range and landing up on the ground; and the need for us to learn to actually stay on our feet and not go down to the ground. If the system you're training doesn't factor in those realities, it may be an amazing martial art or sport, but it is probably not preparing you for a real life or death encounter.

In cultures and countries where people carry firearms or other defensive tools, we need to be very careful of not becoming too dependent on these tools or ignoring them because they are unpalatable based on our own norms. As an example of these dependencies – *We have found in having trained thousands of law-enforcement officers over the years, that law enforcement officers feel most confident when they have their side arms and tools on them. Take them away and unfortunately, that confidence fades tremendously. This creates a level of intense vulnerability and is a very negative consideration in the way we train and develop our protectors.*

We should strive to not become dependent on any specific tool, but adopt what's sometimes referred to as the 'one mind, any weapon approach', where you are the weapon itself and whatever you utilize in your hands may be a tool. For example, *if I am hitting, with open hand strikes, then my hand is the tool. If I have a baton or another type tool and I'm using that, that is the tool. In extreme circumstances, if I had a firearm, then I've got an amazing tool that enables me to do significant damage with minimum effort on my side but I am still the weapon as I operate the tool.*

Understanding and applying tools is a useful concept, particularly when we start looking at defensive items that may be used around us to defend ourselves and taking into consideration that improvised weapons, could also be used by attackers to try and harm you. By understanding these different tools and different options, you should be better able to prepare yourself to effectively fight if you have to. In terms of summarizing some hard truths on this concept, if your system of self-defense doesn't factor in adrenal response realities, doesn't focus on aspects such as simple techniques, gross motor skill functions and what we refer to as forgiving techniques, techniques that allow you to make mistakes because they are simple and efficient, you may land up trying something that sounds and seems wonderful in the gym or dojo, but may have very little benefit for you when it truly comes to fighting for your life.

From your own perspective, no matter how good your personal instructor is, I can almost guarantee he or she won't be there when you need them most. Therefore, it really comes down to your own practical evaluation of what you believe your body can do and what sort of skills and techniques you can be trained to perform. We often think that martial arts and self-defense is something that young people do, but the reality is, as you get older, you actually become an easier target and a more attractive victim for criminals. As an older person, the need for you to learn self-defense and be able to defend yourself is actually more important than for somebody younger who may be a less likely target for that very reason. However, we need to take into account the fact that many of the techniques taught to younger people may not be able to be applied in the same way or structure by older people. The same reality applies to those who are disabled or injured who are also likely to be perceived as an easy and attractive target by people with ill intent.

When we look at the ability to fight if we had to, one thing seems clear from all my research and experience to date, that when looking at the aspects of aggression and commitment – often referred to as attributes – somebody who is aggressive, committed and truly wants to win is more likely to beat somebody who is not as committed, not as aggressive or does not have as much focus. This is true even if the non-aggressive and non-committed person has better technique or more options available. In short, *commitment* and *aggression* generally trump and overcome technique alone. If you don't have time and you don't have the ability to go out and train for an extended period of time, know that just by fighting with all you have got, your chances of survival can be dramatically increased. Having said that, we should still be aware that someone who has the right attributes (commitment and aggression) as well as technique will clearly have the advantage.

Also remember, in many circumstances, with the exception of attacks such as terrorist or active shooter situations, where the wolf, who is committing the attack has already made up their mind that they will sacrifice their own life to commit the attack, your job is not necessarily to beat or stop the attacker but to get the attacker to feel that they've made a mistake and what they thought was easy prey is, in actual fact, not. In the thousands of incidents we've dealt with over the years, we've found that this approach and strategy is highly effective. Just by understanding that in the majority of cases all you need to do is to try to make it hard enough so that your attacker aborts, makes the ability to motivate your fight response more effective. Remember, it's not your job to restrain, control and apprehend (unless you are a law enforcement officer, security profes-

> YOUR PRIMARY OBJECTIVE IS TO KEEP YOU AND YOUR FAMILY SAFE. IN MOST CASES – ALL YOU'VE GOT TO DO IS GET THE PERSON TO STOP THE ATTACK SO YOU CAN GET AWAY.

sional or military person) whose objectives may not be that of escaping, but rather apprehending or stopping an attacker.

Your primary objective is to keep you and your family safe. All you've got to do is get the person to stop the attack so you can get away. Whatever we do from a defensive perspective should be aligned to that objective. As we said earlier when looking at violence, there are only two reasons people ever fight—ego or survival. If we have firmly entrenched our response to focus on survival-based reasoning only and have eliminated ego based motivations, then all we need to make sure of is that we fight with all of the commitment required to survive.

Chapter summary

In summary, when it comes time to action, we need to be able to understand and apply the following:

- The run, hide, fight and communicate approach linked to avoiding/ preventing, deflecting, intercepting or cooperating response options.

- We need to understand and be able to apply the tools of adrenal response management (A.R.M).
- We need to understand the OODA loop and how it works.
- We need to understand the basis for non-physical aggression and de-escalation.
- We need to understand that without base situational awareness and without an understanding of the way that most attacks may happen, the ability for us to respond instinctively and reflexively in an effective manner may be very slim.

By not being able to apply the above, your odds of survival are dramatically reduced should you be exposed to a worst-case scenario. If you think of real and likely situations, you may not be fighting just to protect yourself, you may actually have to take into account your family members or other people around you.

It is very important to factor in the strategy of cooperation. If it is a crime or an attack where you believe cooperating is the right strategy, then you need to understand that being able to control your adrenalin, show the attacker that your aim is to cooperate and in essence, assist them in achieving their objectives so that they leave as quickly as possible without causing you further harm, needs to be the primary driver of what you do. This in itself takes a lot of forethought, practice and rehearsal because the ability to maintain a fight or flight instinct and do the right thing by not giving the attacker a reason to hurt you, is truly something that's much easier said than done.

The truth is that no instructor, book, manual or approach could ever tell you when and when not to fight or draw the line in the sand as to when and how you would respond. As stated previously, if you haven't considered the fact that you might only have 0.3 of a second available to make up your mind as to what to do and when to do it, then you may be leaving your response to a randomized instinctive response – which may be the wrong response to the situation you are in or even lead to freeze and panic.

We also need to understand the fundamentals aspects of legal consequences. Obviously, legalities and laws differ from region to region and country to country. There are really and truly no universal guidelines that apply all over the world. Having said that, in terms of looking at the consequences or baseline actions from our perspective, we should understand that there will always be repercussions to the way you respond to a situation. You need to evaluate what those repercussions could be. Whether those repercussions include you going to hospital, you being potentially physically injured for the rest of your life or maybe even killed, or whether it involves you potentially having to take someone else's life and dealing with the aftermath and consequences thereof, are very complex issues and need to be considered carefully ahead of time. This is important because there really isn't much time for such consideration when an actual attack occurs.

Your objective and your goals need to be to at least draw your own lines in the sand and to work out when and when not to fight or resort to violence in defense of you, your family or others. Remember earlier in this book where we mentioned that if you aren't around, who will be there to protect your family? We should seriously consider such realities when we determine how to respond. I know, for example, that my baseline response is if I truly thought I was going to die anyway or my family would be harmed, I would not hesitate in harming the other person to protect myself and those I love. The reality of this response legally may hinge on what is often referred to as the 'reasonable person' test. The law in many places will compare you and your response to people similar to you. Therefore, in my case, the law would compare me to somebody who was an experienced martial artist, risk, security professional, which means I would probably be judged to a different standard than your average everyday person who may not have such skills and training – this does not deter my response but rather informs it.

In assessing these different variables, we need to understand that you will most likely have to account for your actions or indeed bear the consequences of your non-action. However, if you do not act because of indecision, panic or fear, you may not be alive to defend your actions. The reality is if you think there is a fair chance you may not make it out of a situation alive, what do you have to lose by fighting? If there's no

SIMPLY PUT, RATHER BE IN A POSITION TO SPEND MONEY ON LEGAL FEES THAN HOSPITAL FEES: RATHER BE ALIVE TO TELL YOUR SIDE OF THE STORY, THAN PAUSE OR HESITATE FOR FEAR OF HARMING SOMEBODY ELSE, AND GET HARMED OR KILLED YOURSELF.

other option and you couldn't run and you couldn't hide or you have already tried to run and you have already tried to hide, you may be forced to defend yourself, in which case the after action explanation and use of force becomes a survival necessity – not a choice.

In terms of what is minimum, appropriate or proportionate force – there are many definitions for this. The simple version is that the minimum or the appropriate amount of force used must cease once a situation is under control. Once you understand this key issue, you need to translate it practically which unfortunately is a very complex matter.

If we understand the situations that soldiers, police officers and security professionals face every day when they may have to apply force in self-defense or in the conducting of their duties, the realities are intense, simply because of the limited timeframes available to make decisions on what action should be taken. In reality, you may, in a best case scenario, at most, have a few seconds to decide your actions and the consequences thereof, whereas courts and prosecutors have months to prepare and pull apart every single choice, decision or action that you may have taken.

This may sound complex, but here is an example… *Imagine you are in your car and you have stopped at a traffic light. You are scanning your environment and are extra aware because you know of carjackings that have occurred in this particular area. As you look up you, see what looks to be a 16 or 17-year-old young man with a hoodie pulled really low, running*

*at you with his hand behind his back. You have to respond very quickly.
Your choices are quite simple. Do you put your foot down on the accelerator
and run over what may be a hijacker or do you wait to see what develops?*

Let's examine just a few possible outcomes:

- *Option one: You decide to put your foot down and run him down. You
  look back and there's an old lady leaning over her son in the street, who
  was in fact running to her because he was late. Now you've run him
  over and may have killed him.*
- *Option two: You adopt the same strategy and put your foot down and
  drive over the attacker. As you drive off, he pulls out his gun and he
  starts shooting at you. You realize that if you hadn't run him over, you
  may very well have been killed because somebody who is willing to
  shoot at you as you drive away is likely to be somebody that may be
  predicated to violence and may actually have severely harmed you had
  you not run him down.*
- *Option three: You wait to see what happens and he simply runs past
  your car with no impact.*
- *Option four: Before you can pull off the man pulls his gun out and
  forces you out of the car, beats you and drives off.*

As you can see from such a simple scenario, that with only a few
options provided, even though there may be hundreds of choices available, the consequences of each choice can be very dramatic.

In short, the more we prepare and the more we think about the
consequences and program our actions, the more we understand this
concept of minimum force and the more we understand that we should
only respond with force if it is a necessity in order to survive and we
were left with no choice. We can then better understand and explain
the consequences of our actions. Simply put, rather be in a position to
spend money on legal fees than hospital fees: rather be alive to tell your
side of the story, than pause or hesitate for fear of harming somebody
else, and get harmed or killed yourself…

CHAPTER 6

Consequences and Aftermath

Aftermath – introduction

After any stressful and traumatic incident – whether an argument or a life and death situation – we have to deal with the aftermath and consequences. This could be as simple as deep breathing to slow down your heart rate and manage adrenal response, to complex triage and after-action response. In line with our before during and after (BDA) model, we now need to spend some time looking at the After aspect.

Once you have had to take action, to hopefully avoid or manage a situation, we need to look at the post event actions and appropriate responses. Let's consider these in a few different scenarios and see how they may work.

As previously highlighted in our BDA approach, ideally, we should be applying 80% of our energy towards being proactive and focussed on identifying, ahead of time, potentially dangerous or hazardous situations and making ourselves a hard target, or better still, removing ourselves out of harm's way. Our primary response should be to communicate suspicious action or potentially harmful environmental issues proactively to the relevant authorities. Over years of observations, we have seen that very often people don't pass on such information because they feel it's difficult to quantify – they say things such as *"well, how would I explain it? It was a gut feeling."* It's hard to put a tangible reality to it. This hesitation and reasoning can be easily overcome. The truth is that authorities would rather have over reporting of information than none at all. It is here that we can do our part for our community, our colleagues and other people in general, towards enhancing the overall safety of our community and greater society. In addition, we need to be very aware of the 'Bystander Effect' where we don't take any after action and inform the authorities because we think that other people will be doing this… Don't ever assume that someone else has taken action and informed the authorities – take the effort to do it yourself. In the worst case its double reporting which in the big scheme of things is a non-issue.

When you see something, say something! If you see something suspicious, call the police or notify the authorities. Even if for some reason they may fail to act, or you don't have confidence in their response capability, it's likely that the information you pass on will be recorded somewhere. This aspect is important as if people were diligent in passing on this sort of information, it would enable police or authorities to better plan for the way they proactively mitigate and manage violence or potential crime in any given area. This may even be something as simple as reporting a water leak which could prevent someone having a car accident and is overall, good for the environment anyway.

It's common knowledge that many terrorist and criminal incidents are avoided or prevented through somebody passing on some sort of information ahead of time to the authorities, enabling them to conduct an investigation, and hopefully act in time to

THE BASIC PREMISE IS ONCE YOU BECOME 'ACTIVATED' AND UNLEASH THE INNER SHEEPDOG AND ARE UTILIZING YOUR EYES AND EARS WITH A REAL AWARENESS AND ASSESSMENT CAPABILITY, PASSING RELEVANT INFORMATION ON TO PEOPLE WHO ARE PAID TO KEEP YOU SAFE, YOU ARE A CRITICAL CONTRIBUTOR IN WORKING TOWARDS A SAFER WORLD.

prevent a potential attack or incident. Once again, the basic premise is once you become 'activated' and unleash the inner sheepdog and are utilizing your eyes and ears with a real awareness and assessment capability, passing relevant information on to people who are paid to keep you safe, you are a critical contributor in working towards a safer world.

With regards to which specific details we should look for and try and remember to pass on, include the following: details of your surrounds or location; what you thought was suspicious; descriptive factors about potential suspects – not just the color of clothing – but specific details such as tattoos or identifying marks and even details such as the shoes they were wearing are important. People may quickly change jackets or shirts or other clothing, but they very rarely change things like jewelry or shoes. Details like this become most useful in helping to identify people for the authorities and assist them in providing descriptions for first responders. The more specific you can be upfront, the more benefit the authorities will gain in trying to apprehend or identify people who you thought were suspicious.

Immediate after-action considerations

Immediate after action considerations can vary dramatically based on the situation and your response. You should also realize from a practical perspective, that if you have to look at your own immediate after-action responses, depending on what you did, these would generally include making sure first and foremost, that you scan your environment to determine that there are no secondary or additional threats. It doesn't help that you think you have avoided a situation, but then simply run into another one that may be even worse. *A good example may be you running away from potentially violent attackers into the middle of the road and then getting hit by a car. We need to really factor in safety as our primary and overarching consideration.*

Once you have determined that your immediate environment is safe, even if it's just for a short period of time, the next consideration would be to ensure that you, and those around you, are physically and mentally ok. As soon as you know that you are unlikely to incur any further harm, the appropriate aftercare should be applied. This could include calming people down who are around you and if necessary administering first aid. Providing basic first response medical support and first aid, such as putting pressure on bleeding wounds or providing CPR if you had to, may quite literally save lives. It is important to remember that this should not be done at the expense of your own safety because, if you're not paying attention while you're giving someone else CPR and get hurt or worst case even killed, that's two deaths instead of one! Your situational awareness, pre-planning together with all the tools discussed in this book should hopefully assist and enable you to make the right call in terms of priorities and effective response.

IF YOU HAD TO USE FORCE AND ARE STILL NOT SURE THAT YOU MIGHT HAVE DONE THE CORRECT THING, WE STRONGLY RECOMMEND THAT YOU CALM DOWN AND SEEK LEGAL COUNSEL BEFORE PROVIDING A SWORN STATEMENT OF EVENTS.

With regard to reporting incidents, remember that because of the way we recall incidents – designed to minimize recall trauma for us – and because of the effects of adrenal response, you may not be able to provide an accurate statement straight after an incident. If you are very flustered or you're confused, and especially, if you had to use force and are still not sure that you might have done the correct thing, we strongly recommend that you calm down and seek legal counsel before providing a sworn statement of events. You need to make sure that you recall things properly before providing a statement because anything you say could be taken out of context and may actually get you into trouble, as opposed to highlighting what you actually may have done to protect yourself and others. It's important to give yourself the time just to reflect and to understand what you have been through before you share critical pieces of information that could have significant legal consequences. Obviously having said that, if you have critical information that could lead to the safety of others and the arrest of potentially dangerous people, you should do your best to assist and cooperate with authorities wherever and as soon as possible.

Longer term – aftermath considerations

Despite our focus on proactive prevention and safety, the next level we looked at is the reality of whether you actually may have to run, or have to hide or to fight, and how you then need to look at the various aftermath and consequential possibilities. The first is as a result of sustained adrenal response. It's important to remember that you are not responsible for crime and violence. Even if you are in a situation that you thought was avoidable, the fact is that there are just some situations that cannot be avoided, no matter how much energy and planning you've invested into avoidance and prevention.

With regards to 'after incident recovery', you need to understand this concept and the sooner you can accept this and not blame yourself, the better. Remember, you are not responsible for crime, violence, terrorism or the negative behavior of others. It's not your fault that people do bad things. Talking about the incident, seeking professional help and counseling are very valuable recovery tools and can have a dramatic effect in terms of your psychological well-being and ability to bounce back. Understanding that you may experience continued post adrenal response signs and symptoms such as nervousness, sweating, increased heart rate, being over emotive, being distant, etc. These issues may come to the fore after a traumatic incident. By understanding these possible effects and preparing for them in advance, hopefully you will then be able to deal with them in a practical and realistic way should they manifest.

From an aftermath perspective, you also may find that if you had to fight, or if people were hurt, you may be faced with intensive self-introspection, which occurs whether you win or lose and you may feel doubt and question yourself as to whether you did or did not do the right thing. Men in particular, often feel inadequate or question their responses if they actually were able to avoid a situation and walk away or were defeated in a physical interaction. This is sometimes referred to as the 'black dog'.[1] Knowing that these sorts of emotions – which are often after effects of adrenalin and trauma – are real and may affect you, helps you prepare and enables you to cope with them more effectively.

UNDERSTANDING THE BASICS OF STRESS MANAGEMENT IS A CRUCIAL COMPONENT TOWARDS LEADING A MORE FULFILLED, HEALTHIER, AND SAFE LIFE.

Understanding the basics of stress management is a crucial component towards leading a more fulfilled, healthier, and safer life. While, luckily, in most modern first world societies we are probably safer than humankind has ever been before in terms of direct threats, we are, however, still consistently exposed to stress and trauma on an on-going basis. Some basic stress-coping tools are valuable in terms of being able to perform effectively. Tools like remembering to give yourself a break every now and again so that you can unwind; trying to get enough sleep; making an effort to eat more healthily; making sure you're hydrated and drink water not just soft drinks; making sure you exercise regularly; having regular conversations and human interactions with people you care about (which is becoming less common in todays networked and online world); and having a social circle that enables you to share issues

---

[1] For further reading on the subject, I recommend some of Geoff Thompson's work – see Reference Section.

of concern to you all become critical stress-coping mechanisms. This includes aspects such as:

- Making sure you have regular digital detox's and that our devices work for us and not the other way around.
- Making sure that you drive 'mindfulness' and focus on being present in your own life and not taking wonderful life experiences for granted because we are distracted by all of the inputs we have around us in our complex worlds.

If you are able to manage you stress effectively, you are more likely to make better decisions and cope with the effects of intense situations and their consequences more effectively. This is an evolution of applying ongoing risk management and risk intelligence in all aspects of your life.

The ability to be able to pause and reflect is another tool that can help you manage stress in your day-to-day life. This topic itself has been addressed in many other publications, but you should remember that life, and the art of living, are not theoretical subjects. No book on personal safety and risk management could be complete without addressing your overall strategy for managing stress and living a healthy, safe and fulfilled life.

One last consideration

As unpleasant as it may be, there might be times when, no matter how careful you are, you will end up being a victim of crime in one form or another. This is a harsh reality which is clearly evident in modern society. No book or person can guarantee your absolute security all of the time. As mentioned earlier in this book, sometimes bad things happen to good people. The problem is that being a victim does not only affect you physically, but also psychologically, mentally and emotionally. It is recommended that, should you ever have been a victim of crime or terrorist incident, you seek immediate professional help, i.e. someone reputable who is qualified and has experience in working with trauma victims. Remember that the purpose of any trauma counselling is to restore your inner locus of control, i.e. move you from a victim mentality back to a state of mind where you have integrated the incident into your new worldview. If we see a criminal / terrorist attack as a crisis, we can define such a crisis as:

"An acute response to an event wherein:

- *Psychological homeostasis (balance) has been disrupted;*
- *One's usual coping mechanisms have failed;*
- *There are signs and/or symptoms of distress, dysfunction, or impairment."*[2]

We'll now look at some typical signs and symptoms that some people who have experienced trauma in some form or other typically experience. It is called *Traumatic Stress*, and is totally normal given what you have just survived or gone through. In professional circles, this will only really become a problem should these signs and symptoms persist for a period of more than a month following the incident, or cause severe distress that impinges on everyday functioning to a significant degree.

The trauma/criminal incident survivor may experience the following:

- Recurrent, involuntary, and intrusive distressing memories of the traumatic event(s);
- Recurrent distressing dreams in which the content and/or emotions experienced in the dream are related to the traumatic event(s);
- Dissociative reactions (e.g. flashbacks) in which you as the individual feels or acts as if though the traumatic event(s) were recurring;
- Intense or prolonged psychological distress at exposure to internal or external cues that symbolize or resemble an aspect of the traumatic event(s);

---

[2]See Reference section – Caplan (1961 and 1964).

- Persistent and exaggerated negative beliefs or expectations about oneself or others;
- Exaggerated startle response, e.g. you get a fright more easily at loud noises than you did before,
- Changes in sleeping patterns, i.e. sleeping too much, battling to fall asleep or to stay asleep;
- Hypervigilance;
- Reckless or self-destructive behavior, etc.

Please keep in mind that if you are experiencing any of these above-mentioned points, does not mean you are weak or a failure. What you are going through is *normal* when you take into consideration the very *abnormal* situation(s) you've survived. When looking for a counsellor or psychologist, keep the following guidelines in mind:

- Do they specialize in trauma?
- Do they have formal qualifications in the field of trauma treatment?
- Does he/she have a good reputation in the field of trauma treatment?
- How much does a session cost?
- How long is a treatment session?
- Are they part of a network of trauma counsellors, including medical funds/aids?

Working through trauma takes time. Make sure to factor your family into the healing process. Have a good, reliable support system who will not blame you for what happened. Finally, every trauma will leave a scar. You will never be the same after surviving a traumatic event. You will carry the scars for the rest of your life. But scars are evidence of healing! Only you can decide whether you are going to cling to a victim mentality, or choose to become a survivor. Yes, you went through a horrible situation, but you came out the other side. You survived. Don't allow anyone to take that fact away from you.

Conclusion

It is my sincere wish that many of the models discussed in this book should hopefully be of value to you. Nobody knows how you retain information, or how your brain is wired, better than you. You should feel free to change, adjust, modify or reframe any of the content, in a way that you would remember and apply it. This is important, because at the end of the day, no matter what content is in this book, you won't have this book in front of you and you won't be able to page to the different sections to remind yourself what to do when you need to respond to an extreme situation.

By accepting the reality of the world you live in, working on making your responses instinctive and reflexive, by being realistic about what you can do and by putting just a little bit of effort into your own personal safety and family safety preparation, you can quite literally make yourself a hard target. The benefit of being a hard target is that hopefully, due to the victim selection process, you will not be selected by predators out there and never have to manage a worst-case situation.

Your aim should be to enjoy life to its fullest, and participate as a valid contributor to society, where you actually help enhance the safety of your fellow citizens by becoming practical eyes and ears for the authorities. This is critical as when we look at the way that crime and terrorism are evolving – we all need to be part of the solution.

At a base level, at the very least if you should have the confidence and capability to protect yourself and your family. You should understand some of the primary issues that can cause concern and anxiety and how to manage them in a practical way. If you understand how the media propagates and shares information, and are not distracted by what appears to be reality but may actually just be 'noise', you can avoid paranoia and focus on reality. By using your Awareness Toolbox which includes practical tools such as base-lining, intuition, the 3PC-S and color codes required to actually determine where we are vulnerable, how vulnerable we are, and we need to do to mitigate that vulnerability, we can truly enhance our own personal safety in a very proactive manner. In the worst case, the ability to apply Adrenal Response Management (A.R.M), develop and apply Planned Incident Actions (PIA's) and understand how the Run, Hide, Fight and Communicate (RHFC) approach may work, could hopefully assist you to survive worst case scenarios – if they actually happen. You should remember that you have to apply skills in all aspects of your life – work, personal and virtual. We are all spending more and more time online and our virtual presence continues to grow and expand, and as such, our approach to securing ourselves online should be expanding and improving in line with this.

We should strive to ensure that we do as much as possible beforehand, based on the fact, that with some situations, you just can't come back from them. The ability to mitigate an attack, minimize the impact of that attack or, hopefully make sure that at worst, you are still alive to tell the story, is an important skillset for the modern era. We can no longer just delegate that responsibility to law enforcement and other government agencies. We cannot even totally shift responsibility to private security to do this for us. While all of these role players become valid layers of safety for us and go a long way to enhance our personal safety, the reality is that you become your own bodyguard, develop your own understanding of what to do in worst case scenarios and maintain, at the very least, just a base core understanding of what to do, hopefully you should then be able to go through life without ever having to apply it! The threats are too complex for our Sheepdogs to handle alone, you need to use your inner sheepdog to be part of the solution.

The core concepts of being aware but not afraid, being proactive and empowered and finding the balance to be prepared but not expend energy on perceived issues that may manifest in paranoia is a worthy goal. The challenge is to find the balance, and to understand that all aspects of our lives are interlinked and driving effective behavior in our personal lives, our work lives, and our virtual lives will enhance your overall resilience and wellbeing. Some core principles to remember are summarized below:

- ✓ **Acceptance** – We must accept that we or our families, organizations and people are exposed to risk as a part of life.
- ✓ **Realistic** – We must ensure that we are in touch with what is actually happening and prevent our imaginations from running wild or conversely stay ignorant, living in a state of DENIAL.
- ✓ **Integration** – We must integrate smart risk practices into our everyday lives and organizational structures.
- ✓ **Flexibility** – We must become adaptable to changes that may occur.
- ✓ **Pro-activity** – We must adhere to an attitude of pro-activity and pre-empt any potentially threatening situations.
- ✓ **Logical** – Practical application is more important than perception, there should be a sound basis behind any application or practice.

The challenge we have is in application – we need to do things. It's hard to change behavior but once we have started and have some inertia it's easier to achieve momentum and build good habitual behaviors. Our goal should be to embrace the wonderful opportunities that life has to offer in a meaningful and significant manner. The challenge is to achieve the Dynamic Risk Equilibrium (DRE) where we are adaptable, agile, and resilient so that we can capitalize on opportunity and minimize the potential downside issues, in other words be Risk Intelligent. I would like to cite two of my mentors to close off this book as they have stated things in a beautifully simple way:

Life is a gift!

Dr. Dennis Hanover –
10th Dan, Founder of DSSJ

Do not waste emotions on things you cannot influence!

Major (Ret.) D.M. Sharp –
BEM. HM (P.F. ROK), Comm. M (USA)

I really hope that you never have to resort to having to run, hide, or fight and that by applying the tools outlined in this book, you are able to make yourself an unattractive and hard target and that you are able to identify situations which may be threatening and remove yourself from them before you are exposed, thus enabling you to lead a healthier, safer, and less stressed life.

Sincerely yours in safety and security,

Dr. Gavriel Schneider

Annexure: Scenarios and Applications

Introduction

In terms of applying the knowledge, concepts, principles, and practices shared with you in this book, it is exceptionally difficult to ensure that you could apply practically, skills that of necessity, can only be explained in a book such as this, in theoretical terms. As discussed in the section on adrenal response management (A.R.M), the requirements to be able to perform effectively are, obviously first and foremost, having some sort of context or understanding of a situation, i.e. situational awareness, which can only be developed through realistic and repetitive training and actual experience. Obviously, to try and develop the correct instinctive response for the correct stimulus or situation, we would need extensive repetition of the right rehearsal and right response to ensure that our fight or flight instincts don't overwhelm our reaction and that we do not freeze or panic. This section can be considered a stand-alone to the rest of the book and whilst it references aspects from within the book, it also covers key issues so that you can use them independently without having to refer back to the relevant section (unless you want to).

This section has been included as a base for considering practical application and is focused on providing some guidelines applicable to common threat based issues along with some recommended actions. It's important to reiterate that as discussed in several places in this book – no instructor or trainer – or book for that matter – can tell you exactly when and when not to fight or use force, in defense of yourself, or others.

Similarly, responses vary dramatically and it is impossible to recommend the perfect response for every scenario derivative. Having said that, if you don't think about it ahead of time, and don't program the correct responses, the likelihood of you doing the right or wrong thing, could hinge on the roll of a dice… When it comes to potentially harming somebody else or you getting harmed, and with the potential for extreme consequences such as jail time for the wrong decision, we must at least give ourselves the best possible chance for making the right choice and implementing the correct action if a situation were to occur.

In order to break this section down, we will look at each different aspect but integrate concepts wherever possible. A good way to understand the idea of applied scenario response training is to think of all the different places you could find yourself where something may go wrong. Looking at this simply, you are likely to potentially be traveling in some mode of transport, be it a motor vehicle, plane or train – maybe even a boat. You may be walking, i.e. on foot, going from one place to another or you may be static at a venue, which may be a place of work, a social environment, like a restaurant, or you may be at your residence.

Generally, if we can cover our base responses to situations that may go wrong in these sorts of environments (mobile in a mode of transport, static at a venue, or on foot), we should be able to ensure for ourselves an overarching plan and structure that should enable the right response to some of the worst-case scenarios. It is also important to remember that as discussed several times in this book, our goal should be to avoid situations that are avoidable and prevent bad things from happening wherever possible. As a result, unless you are a first responder (such as a police, security or military person), we would apply the concept of run, or get away and escape, as our primary option. If this was not achievable, then we should seek to avoid the situation by hopefully hiding and making sure that we weren't hurt. As a worst case, if we're left with no other resort, then fighting is probably the only option available. Please also remember that these responses are dynamic, and you may have to hide first, then fight, and then run or apply these in any other order that the situation may dictate.

PLEASE ALSO REMEMBER THAT THESE RESPONSES ARE DYNAMIC, AND YOU MAY HAVE TO HIDE FIRST, THEN FIGHT, AND THEN RUN OR APPLY THESE IN ANY OTHER ORDER THAT THE SITUATION MAY DICTATE.

This response approach can be used as a basis for planning and responding not just to security-related issues such as vehicular attack or an active shooter situation, but it also has relevance in situations such as fire, or even in terms of natural disasters, such as a building collapse. A good friend of mine was an emergency responder to a major earthquake and commented on how the randomness of where people were hurt and where they were not, seemed to defy logic. People who hid under objects sometimes didn't make it. People who ran sometimes didn't make it. But in other cases, they survived even though the exact same response got someone else killed. Despite the variable of randomness that may seem to dominate responses in these extreme situations, having a cool, calm and collected approach along with a plan, without doubt increases your chances of survival in a worst-case scenario.

Your home

Your home is a very important aspect in terms of security. It is a place where you will spend a lot of time, return to and leave from and have your family there. It is also the place where you are most likely to let your guard down and be in condition white. Let's start off with a simple range of options for this overall complex topic of residential security. For Option one, let's look at a scenario of a residential security incident. When we look at security at the place where we live, we generally get people talking about basically two broad categories – communal living structures (such as apartment blocks) or separate dwellings (standalone houses). These are the two most common broad variations even though there are in between structures such as condos or townhouses.

People often talk, from a security perspective, about the advantages of apartment living vs stand-alone houses. There are differing opinions of which would be the more secure in terms of the common threats i.e. burglary, home invasion, etc. To analyze this, we should look at the basic concept discussed in our Awareness Toolbox – the application of base-lining. If you don't baseline and know what is normal and relevant for a specific area and what is out of the ordinary and what is not, it is exceptionally difficult to figure out whether the area you are living in is safe or not. It's also important to understand that crime trends shift and change. What may be perceived to be a very safe area, may actually encounter a crime spree and not turn out to be a safe area over a short period. Very often, higher income areas are perceived to be safer areas, but because there are many more targets for criminals in wealthy areas then there are in poor areas, they may actually be more attractive hunting grounds.

Without going into the nature the in-depth analysis of crime statistics, area demographic threats and related aspects, which would take up a book in its own right, let's just consider the fundamentals of trying to understand geographically and environmentally what you're looking for when assessing residential security. As per our 3PC-S approach, we need to be able to determine what a safe or unsafe area is. Choosing your area of residence is important. As a starting point, we need to form our baseline, i.e. what makes the areas I am assessing safe or not? From there, choosing your street or specific location would be the next level. What do the neighbors look like? What are the immediate surrounds? Is there anything that would be risky or untenable in that area that may pose an additional risk or threat to me or my family?

If that all looks okay, the next step would be to look at the residence itself. We will deal with houses first and then Apartment building. Let us now apply our defense-in-depth model. We need to assess whether the security of the house seems appropriate and proportionate for the threat environment that we have determined for the area. There is no point putting up extra high walls with electric fencing and a state-of-the-art alarm system if there's never really been a crime problem in the area and if none of the neighbors have such measures. In fact, this may actually create a situation where people would wonder what it is that is being so heavily protected… Taking this into account, we should understand that, at the very least, you would like to make sure that your own security is just a little bit above that of your neighbors. This is not to say you should want to compete with them but what ideally you would like to see happen is that if criminals were applying their attacker ritual and target selection, that they would look at your house and they would think, wow, there's just a little bit extra security there. Maybe there's an extra wall. Maybe there's better lighting. Maybe there are signs that say there is an alarm. Maybe you and your family just appear to be more vigilant or you have a dog. All of those things add up, becoming layers in our defense-in-depth approach which may cause a criminal to rather choose another house. The more layers you have, the less likely you are to be targeted.

Unfortunately, with every security issue, there is an embedded compromise and a down side. As you secure your house, the security measures may add some level of inconvenience for you and your family. In addition, as mentioned, there is always also a small minority of criminals who may ask – why have you gone to the effort of applying measures to protect your house – there must be something valuable inside! Despite these complexities, they are not enough of a reason to ignore security. If we assume that we may get broken into, burgled or be targeted by criminals for whatever reason, we can disempower ourselves and, in essence, become sitting ducks and vulnerable to attack at any given period without applying measures to protect ourselves and our property. A base level of acceptance empowers us to be able to act and lead a safe and healthier existence. Security should always be a balanced approach and if we are too anxious, or feel too inconvenienced in considering the actual likelihood of something occurring, then we have gone too far with security.

In terms of worst-case scenarios, one of the variables from a residential security and quality of life perspective is to ensure that we also look for and assess general safety issues and hazards. We'd like to know what happens if, for example, the electricity goes out? Is the wiring reliable and safe? Is the actual physical and structural design of the house well-constructed? It doesn't help if you buy a house in what you perceive to be the safest area, but then have walls collapse and injure you. It's also quite important that we think about and analyze worst case scenarios such as fire hazards, or even potential flooding, depending on where you live, as it is pointless to look just at security in isolation. The goal is your safety and security from as many different threats as possible. Threats should never be limited to only criminal or terrorist activities. It is important to appreciate how comprehensive your preparation should be.

It is also important to understand that the more we secure our house to keep people out, in essence, the more we lock ourselves in. If that's the case, our escape/run option becomes a very difficult task to implement. If we are over secured, we may only be left with the option of sheltering inside and if that did not work, worst case would be fighting for our safety. If this is the situation, your goal is to try and set up as many barriers as you can to delay potential attackers or assailants who are trying to harm you, slow them down or stop them from being able to get to you and your family so that hopefully responders, such as police officers or security, could get there in time before intruders would be able to harm you.

This may involve implementing actions such as separating out living areas from sleeping areas. It may also involve setting up a safe or a holding room, which may not necessarily be as dramatic as it sounds. Simply placing an outside (external) door on an inside en-suite bathroom with a bolt lock may be enough to buy you an extra few minutes if intruders were to gain access to your house.

In terms of apartment complexes versus houses, obviously the core concept of 'more' comes into play, more people, more eyes, more ears and a unified approach to security, would certainly contribute to a robust and structured security environment. Having said that, unfortunately, the frustrating downside of this issue is that because there are often so many people there, it's really hard to see who belongs and who doesn't. As a result of this traffic, it may be very difficult to proactively control who enters your immediate space or space around you and who doesn't, which can pose a risk in its own right.

The other issue obviously with high rise or apartment living could be fire risk or similar issues. Think about it – if you are on the 20th floor and a fire breaks out, it may be very difficult for you to get out of the building. One only has to remember the results of what happened to people on the top floors of the Twin Towers during the 9/11 attacks to realize how quickly being high up can become a massive hindrance, issue and safety hazard when compared to being low down enough to be able to get out quickly and efficiently.

In summary, when it comes to residential or home security, applying a defense-in-depth approach to ensure that you, at the very least, have basic hold or run strategies in place, and that practically thinking about what do you need to do, just to make sure that you have your base level of security covered (i.e. just a bit more than your neighbors) is the critical starting point. Making sure you have basic reactive hold or run strategies is an important reactive consideration. In addition, you should strive for the security balance, as I am sure that you would like to try to have your security in an appropriate proportion so that it doesn't impinge on your quality of life in a negative way and that you find an effective balance, that you are on the right side of being proactive and aware, but not paranoid.

Mobile consideration 1 – vehicle security

The next issue we will address is vehicle security. Often, depending on where you live, you will spend an extensive period of time in your vehicle. One of the considerations to bear in mind, and there have been many scientific studies done about this, is that when we sit in our cars, we tend to extend our personal boundaries to that of the vehicle itself. One only has to watch the way people behave when they are stationary at intersections, or driving in their vehicles, to realize that they often don't consider the fact that others can see into the vehicle at any given time. People will sing and may conduct themselves in a manner where they think no one can see them, just because they are in their car!

We should also understand that there are two key aspects to vehicle security – the first is based on protecting the vehicle itself and the assets that may be in it. The aim here is to ensure that the vehicle itself is secured and that it does not get stolen or broken into and your possessions or contents inside removed… The second aspect is to ensure that when you are driving the vehicle, that you are safe. This second aspect leans significantly towards our awareness and being present when we operate our vehicles, i.e. safe driving as well as personal security issues when approaching your car, getting in to it, moving and getting out of it. Both of these aspects have significant security and safety implications.

When looking at these two aspects of vehicle security, you should also take into account the reality (in most locations), that you are far more likely, to get into a traffic accident than actually landing up in a security situation. As such, basic safe driving practices such as wearing your seatbelt, maintaining safe following distances and making sure you stay switched on and in color code yellow as a minimum when you're driving, all become critically important.

If we flashback to that COI triangle where we discussed capability, opportunity and intent – somebody who wants to hijack your vehicle when you are in it or steal your vehicle if the opportunity presented itself, would likely have the capability and intent – which are the two variables you cannot to control. Therefore, we have to focus on the one variable we can – controlling the opportunity!

In addition to the application of basic defensive driving practices which we should apply always, i.e. we assume other people will make mistakes and proactively expect and prepare to manage them as you drive, the objective, from a vehicular security point of view when you're driving, is to ensure that you have continuous movement and leave yourself effective escape route options so that if something went wrong, you could drive away. Remember, from a security perspective, you are more vulnerable when you are stationary or travelling at a slow speed. When you are stationary a person could approach your vehicle before you could drive off. If somebody, for example, threw an item or obstacle in front of the vehicle, it may cause you, at lower speed, to slam on your brakes, whereas at a higher speed, you may swerve to avoid an obstacle or an object and keep going. As such we should raise and lower our awareness in our vehicles as per our speed and environment on an ongoing basis

To try and make sure that you continuously drive in an effective way, one of the things you should remember to do is to get into good driving habits and ensure that you apply security principles as your normal, everyday operational procedure as opposed to something you would do just when you perceive there's a risk or an issue. This links back to pacing yourself and rationing your awareness effectively. For example, you might see a traffic light ahead of you changing color, habitually you may speed up to try and make it through before the light changes. If you don't make it through (which is often the way it lands up), you would not have time to scan the environment, or you may speed up and then have to slam on your brakes at the last instant and be stuck at a traffic light for a longer period, also potentially causing an accident. Instead, driving in a calm and collected manner, rationing your awareness, controlling your speed and options can prevent risk-taking driving, which could get you into trouble.

We often get very rushed and perceive that if we drive faster or drive recklessly, we will get wherever we are going quicker. We tested this perception practically and we have found that polite, efficient and security-type driving on a typical journey of roughly 15 kilometers, usually only adds about 30 seconds of travel time to your journey, so it's truly not an inconvenience issue (even though we perceive it to be). It's more of a mental perception issue. In terms of our perceptions, we may perceive that we control that piece of road in front of us and it's ours and therefore someone cutting in front of us really gets us angry and frustrated – despite the fact that this may only add a second or two onto your journey, which is really not a big deal.

> IF YOU CAN LEAVE ITEMS IN THE TRUNK OF THE CAR, WHERE PEOPLE CAN'T SEE THEM WHEN THEY LOOK INTO YOUR VEHICLE, IT INCREASES THE EFFECTIVENESS OF YOUR ABILITY TO REDUCE EXPOSURE AND REDUCES THE LIKELIHOOD OF SOMEBODY BREAKING INTO YOUR VEHICLE.

By understanding that such a mindset is actually just a mental concept, i.e. in our heads and that by deciding not to think this way we are instantly safer. By not taking the way other people drive personally and being more flexible in terms of accident prevention, and from a security perspective leaving yourself escape routes and reactionary gaps – could make a massive difference to your safety and your peace of mind.

In terms of general vehicle security issues – basics like keeping doors locked, windows up when you see something suspicious or are in a dangerous area – are critical aspects to making you a harder target. Not leaving items easily visible when driving in heavy traffic or a dangerous area is also another layer of deterrence. If you can leave items in the trunk of the car, where people can't see them when they look into your vehicle, it increases the effectiveness of your ability to reduce exposure and reduces the likelihood of somebody breaking into your vehicle.

The worst-case scenario from a vehicular security perspective that most people think about is a carjacking situation. Whilst, generally speaking the carjacker's intent is to get the vehicle, their key risk is that you are there at the time and as such you may get hurt or even taken hostage. If you cannot avoid such a situation, your approach should be to try and give them the vehicle as smoothly and as effectively as possible, ensuring that they realize that your aim is to cooperate and not fight back i.e. not give them a reason to hurt you or take you hostage. Having said that, remember nobody can tell you when and when not to fight. If you thought that you were in a situation from which you weren't going to be able to get out of, obviously, if there was no other choice, you may then resort to fighting or engaging in effective self-defense.

Other considerations around vehicular security hinge specifically on aspects such as – how you approach the vehicle; where you park and what to do as you get into and out of the vehicle. Let's discuss these aspects briefly. In terms of where you park, this would depend, once again, on your risk profile and the area assessment. One useful habit is the idea of starting to implement *flight-ready* parking. Flight-ready parking is practicing reversing into a parking space with the front of the vehicle now facing outward. Whilst this may seem to be a nuisance, and in the beginning, may seem to be frustrating, it enables speedy departure. You should remember that vehicles were designed to be driven forward. With the exception of two blind spots, when you are driving forward, you have maximum visibility. When you reverse, you tend to have only a one -dimensional focus and as such an in-built vulnerability and also minimalistic vehicle handling capability. Flight-ready parking becomes a very useful habit for minimizing risk when pulling off.

Another consideration is parking in well-lit areas that are easily accessed, therefore minimizing the time it takes you to approach and get into the vehicle. It also means that your vehicle is less likely to get broken into or stolen because of regular passing traffic and oversight as people will be able to see your vehicle all the time as they walk to and from their destinations. When you approach your car, you should try and ensure that you approach with the key in your hands ready and that you don't dawdle. You should do a quick scan to see your vehicle is safe and there are no issues before getting in. Your normal approach should be to conduct a basic scan to check that the vehicle is in the position you left it in and whether there are any obstacles that would stop you from moving or driving out effectively or whether there is anything under the vehicle and in general, if anything seems suspicious. Getting in and out of vehicles is a transition and transitions are always an area of vulnerability. When you walk out of a building, say the shopping mall, and you walk towards a vehicle, if you are distracted and not paying attention, you a very vulnerable target. When you pull up in your vehicle at a new place, you should be heightening your awareness as you get out of the vehicle and make your way forward – simply because you are coming from a known into an unknown scenario.

One should also be aware of criminals using jamming technology to override you locking your car or being able to start your car. Unfortunately, it's not too hard to clone automatic starters and remote locking devices but being aware of these issues may help you to mitigate some of the threats. Getting into the habit of not leaving valuables in your vehicle will minimize the inconvenience should your vehicle be stolen.

Mobile consideration 2 – other modes of transport

The consideration of you being a passenger in, or using other modes of transport is the next issue we will discuss. This relates to the fundamentals of basic transport security on other modes of transport such as public transport and includes modes of transport such as busses, trains and even airplanes. As an example, airplane travel is an area where we may feel that we have very limited security and safety influence over. From a safety perspective, we may feel there's very little we can do if a crime was going to be committed or something was going to go wrong while we're in the airplane. This is not necessarily so, and there are a wide range of variables that are under our control. For example, checking the safety record of the airline you're going to fly with is a good starting point…

Another example is that – *seating yourself further back in the plane may also be beneficial as you get to observe all the other passengers and you may be able to notify the air crew if you notice something suspicious or out of the ordinary.* In addition, seating yourself close to escapes and exits also provide you enhanced potential for survival if something goes wrong. We should be especially focused on our arrival and departures when doing long haul flights specifically if we are arriving at locations we are unfamiliar with, being met by someone you can trust is a great security consideration when travelling to new places. Even protecting your luggage by applying basic defense in depth is something most people don't consider, i.e. having bags that are not too expensive and create the perception of wealth, not putting too many personal detail on the bag tags, locking the bags, etc. all become useful security measures.

As another application of principles – let's take a look at busses and trains as examples of public transport. Obviously your first activity should be to vet the safety record of any mode of transport you wish to travel on. If you feel it's safe enough based on the information you can gather aspects such as, having a basic route plan and knowing safe havens along the way is important, even if you are not the driver. A safe haven could be defined as a place where there are lots of people, a place where you are unlikely to be harmed, and where you could get help if necessary. Often safe havens are places like hospitals, police stations, or potentially even foreign embassies or missions in different countries you may be travelling to. You never know what could go wrong and knowing where to go if something does, could be lifesaving in extreme circumstances.

In terms of your route, it's useful, if for example, you are jumping onto a bus or a train, to know a few key landmarks in case you need to jump off at an earlier stop or when something goes wrong. Consider a basic example – *where there may be mechanical issues on the train you're on and you have to get off at a different station to the one planned and need to figure out where you are. You are now in an unfamiliar environment which may become a security hazard.* In examples like this we should also be cognizant that we have become so dependent on technology and often think, 'well I can just call up Google maps or any other app' on your phone and use that to figure out where I am and where I'm going, but when you have no signal or maybe your cellphone's battery is flat, this may not be an option. As with any aspect of security, the basics of planning and awareness become critical issues.

In any crowded public space – protecting your personal space is important but becomes very difficult on public transport. It is important that you try to position yourself where you have good visibility, possibly

KEEP IN MIND THAT ROUTINE SETS YOU UP FOR AN AMBUSH.

with your back to a wall where it's hard for people to sneak up behind you and ideally close to an exit in case you had to get off in a hurry. Making sure your valuables are well protected and kept close to your person and held in such a way that it would be difficult for somebody to grab them from you and run, is also something to think about.

Being able to pick your travel times may not always be possible based on commuter schedules and the distance to travel, but one of the core safety principles that is often taught, is to try and vary your travel routes and times slightly. It's much harder for somebody trying to maintain surveillance on you or trying to gather information about you, to figure out your movements if sometimes you're on an earlier or later train and the same would apply to getting on or off at a different bus or bus stop. These small variances can all add up to your overall target hardening approach. By slightly changing and varying your routine, processes and behaviors, you can make yourself a harder target for a planned criminal attack. As an overarching consideration, when selecting any mode of transport, safety records of the method of transport you choose should be really important.

When it comes to taxis or shared transport such as Uber, safety all depends on where you are and whether, for example, the back section of the vehicle is actually blocked off from the front section. In many countries, fake taxis are a serious issue. While we perceive a taxi is safe because it's a marked vehicle, this may not always be the case. This even more true for rideshares based on App bookings. We suggest that if you don't feel safe, or you're not 100% confident, then try to sit behind the driver, as in extreme circumstances, you would be able to grab him around the face and control him. Another option could be to sit in a place where it would be hard for him to grab you such as diagonally opposite in the back seat. You should also think about sitting on the side of the pavement so if you had to get out quickly, you would not get out into moving traffic. As can be seen, there are many variables to consider and the message here is to actually think about them and not just function on autopilot where if something went wrong, you would be totally unprepared.

Obviously, trying to only select vehicles that are vetted and look safe is a good starting point. If you haven't got that level of comfort (which is not always possible in every country and every circumstance), it is suggested that you find some level of alternate transport instead of taking the risk with an un-vetted, possibly unroadworthy vehicle that, for some reason, is triggering your intuition and telling you that this may not be a safe call. Remember, our intuition is our early warning system. You should trust it and utilize it.

Mobile consideration 3 – transitioning

The area of maximum exposure and vulnerability is often when we transition from one mode of transport to another, or transition from one place to another. *For example, even when in a restaurant, you may have been really careful where you sat – ideally in a place that enabled you to observe who was coming in and coming out or you sat in a place where your back was shielded and protected or in a place where you could access the exits if necessary, you may feel quite secure in this situation but when you walk out, you are coming into an environment that you haven't checked, haven't scanned and it may be totally foreign or new*. Even if it's a place you are familiar with, this is when you should potentially heighten your awareness and switch on. Transitions are very important for overall personal safety.

Adopting the process of applying color codes and the other aspects of your awareness toolbox, and focusing on staying in color yellow would enable you to potentially heighten your awareness, possibly to an orange, if you were walking into a situation where you had no comfort or prior knowledge. You can always quickly move down to yellow if there's no threat whatsoever. However, if you continuously exist in a state of white, you are exceptionally vulnerable – especially during the transition phase.

Staying safe on foot

Now that we've discussed the basics of residential and Mobile security, let's talk about security when you are on foot and also assess some issues related to being at different venues or places that you may not be familiar with. As highlighted on several occasions, one of the core issues with personal security comes down to applying basic awareness. Whilst we've spent a lot of time discussing aspects and tools such as the three-point-check system, as well as understanding and assessing your environment, after we've been able to come up with some level of base-lining, it is critically important for us to understand how we can control our own personal space.

The unfortunate reality, once we factor in the 21 foot/7-meter rule, is that it's really hard for you to have an effective spatial barrier in terms of defending yourself from a direct threat. One of the things you need to be able to do is try and apply your ability to forecast attacker-ritual (the understanding of the way criminals pick and approach targets) so that you can target-harden yourself and ideally not get selected in the first place.

Unfortunately, the complexity is such that on foot, there are many things that may go wrong. The simple limitation of not having eyes in the back of your head makes it quite easy for people to approach from the back if you are not alert. Let's discuss a few of these potential negative events so that we can assess the appropriate proactive measures and relevant response options. Among the most common threat issues is that you may be faced with some sort of robbery situation, where the attacker may be armed with a knife or gun. Generally speaking, when in an armed robbery situation, the attacker wants to get something off you. Their objective is to gain an asset, be it a cellphone, a watch or something else. Much like a carjacking, your strategy, if you weren't able to prevent or avoid the situation in the first place, and you're quite confident that this person doesn't want to necessarily kill, assault or abduct you but just wants an object, is generally to be as cooperative as possible. To give them what they're after as efficiently as possible to limit the likelihood of them hurting you is the primary strategy. Trying to make it as simple and as effective as possible by keeping your movements slow and transparent, showing your willingness to cooperate, avoiding eye contact and making sure you listen to and follow instructions are some of the basics to remember.

The next threat aspect which may evolve from a robbery or manifest on its own is the issue of assault (unarmed or armed). The issue with an assault, when you are unable to avoid it, brings us to that inherently difficult decision point – DO YOU FIGHT BACK or NOT. When it comes to complex decision points like this, particularly under stress, it is exceptionally hard to ensure we will make the right decision in the very limited time available to make it. If you do decide to defend yourself, one of the critical action points is that you have got to make sure you have a reflexive understanding and intuitive response capability of being able to switch on aggression and be able to fight when necessary, even if you feel your flight response is overwhelming you. Using the first two aspects of our ARM tools; 1-Realistic training and experience and

2-Visualization and mental role play, can help to prepare you for this and improve the likelihood of correct response.

This capability is particularly relevant where the threat you are facing may not be an armed robbery, but may actually be a kidnapping, or an abduction and the assailant is planning to remove you from your current location and take you somewhere else. Generally speaking, with kidnapping and abductions, the attacker is more prone to use violence and likely to cause more damage early on when they're trying to assert their authority. Whilst the initiation phase of such an incident is very sensitive because of this issue, the difficult variable to remember is that once you are moved from the location where you are kidnapped from, to a secondary location, after which you're likely to be moved to yet another location, the chances of being rescued and found diminish tremendously.

As such, whilst one of the guiding principles for an armed robbery – is that it is best to apply a strategy of cooperation, this does not necessarily apply to a kidnapping. If people were trying to kidnap you, most likely you may need to resort to fighting and escaping as quickly as possible, simply because of the fact that once you have been removed from your initial location, the chance of survival and rescue decreases significantly. If you were unable to escape in the early stages, strategies such as humanization (whereby …. And make them think of you as a person) – understanding the Stockholm syndrome (where you are … and side with your kidnappers) and as such can recognize this and prevent it are important aspects of coping and surviving. Probably the most critical aspect is the application of mental resilience tools and positive mental mindset reinforcement which need to come into play whilst waiting for rescue or planning an escape.

If we look at the threat of armed assault from a firearm perspective, one of the critical things to understand is what sort of weapon is being used and what is the damage that this weapon can inflict. This is often difficult to determine unless you are an expert. However, a base understanding, for example, of what sort of cover is effective from a 9 mm semi-automatic pistol as compared to an AK47 assault rifle, could make a fundamental difference to your options and ability for hide and escape.

Once again, if it's an armed hold-up and the attacker hasn't hurt anyone, they probably want something. Cooperation then becomes the valid strategy. If it gets to the point where the assailant starts shooting or is close to you and you feel you're going to get killed, what do you have to lose by engaging in some sort of self-defense initiative? This leads on to active-shooter/active armed assailant scenarios i.e. the worst-case attacks where we have a clear understanding that this person's objective is to kill us and the people around us.

The concept that one or two armed attackers can potentially assault or kill lots of people – maybe tens, twenties or even hundreds is quite a scary consideration. Whilst we have touched on some of these issues in Chapter 5, if applying a RHFC (Run, Hide, Fight and Communicate) approach, at some point we need to look for a window of opportunity where the attacker's gun may jam or they may have to change magazines. We must also remember the adrenal response function, where this attacker is very likely to be inhibited by adrenal dump too and will have tunnel vision, auditory exclusion and all those other variables, which may allow us to be able to approach, from a blind spot, and physically incapacitate the attacker.

One of the effective principles in any active attacker situations along with our RHFC methodology is to ensure that we don't engage unarmed if we couldn't run or hide. Finding improvised weapons or defensive tools in our environment is a critical aspect of our environmental scan incorporated in our three-point-check system (3PC-S). In addition, if you were in an active attacker situation and had been able to pre-rehearse with your colleagues, techniques such as 'swarming' – whereby numerous people charge the attacker simultaneously from different angles – become very effective. In applying approaches such as 'Swarming' there is no doubt that people are going to get shot and hurt, but this would happen anyway. As such, the importance of being able to attack the attacker as soon as possible can't be over emphasized!

Obviously in an environment where the carrying of firearms is legal, the ability for people to engage and neutralize the attacker/s as quickly as possible is critical. If you are in an environment where it's legal to carry a firearm and you are somebody who does carry a firearm or a Sheepdog who carries one in the line of duty, there's a tremendous responsibility that comes with this which is often neglected. Understanding how to engage with your firearm at close quarters when somebody is shooting back at you where there are innocent people around you and the pressure is intense is only the beginning – actually being able to act and function instinctively under these extreme circumstances is critical. This is a vastly different situation from shooting at a non-moving paper target where the only pressure might be time constraints when engaging multiple paper targets in a preset sequence. This is obviously not the ideal preparation for engaging criminals/terrorists in real life, up close and personal. Joining a local firearm academy where *combat shooting* is taught and might be very beneficial.

As such, I believe it to be critically important that if you are somebody who wants to carry a firearm, you need to take the necessary steps to ensure you are responsible, accountable and capable of utilizing that weapon, otherwise you may as well not have it at all. In fact, research has shown that if the weapon is not already in your hand when the engagement begins, the drawing process, if it's not second nature, is often the inhibiting factor and stops effective use. Many people get shot or killed whilst they're trying to draw their weapon in response to situations because they have not made this process instinctive.

One of the other important aspects to remember, when we talk about responding to armed robberies or active attack situations is to have a plan that's shared between yourself and others who may be exposed should something occur beforehand i.e. proactively. If we leave this aspect to the last minute, the way people respond will be totally random. Some people may do the right thing, while others may freeze, and others may panic and others may run. If everybody discussed what the appropriate reaction should be, rehearsed and drilled it, we are more likely to perform effectively and minimize the negative consequences of a worst-case scenario.

One of the last threat scenarios to consider when on foot, and that is often raised as a concern, particularly for females, is sexual assault and sexual intimidation. While, once again, this topic is probably the subject of an entire book in its own right, it's critically important for us to have some base-level understanding of the way these attacks usually happen. When we look at sexual assault and rape, most statistical information shows that the majority of sexual assault and rapes actually occur from somebody who the victim knows and was usually comfortable enough to be alone with. This may seem contrary to the random attack situation that most people perceive is the biggest threat which, whilst I am not saying this won't happen, is not the most common way these attacks occur. One of the concepts of prevention is making sure you are very careful who you are alone with and that when you are alone, other people know where you are and that you control your personal space and that wherever possible, you ensure that there are boundaries between you and people around you.

This basic level of self-protection should become second nature, and in itself, is often a significant enough deterrent, because people who carry themselves with confidence, are less likely to be selected as targets in the first place. However, one of the important things to understand with sexual assault is that as a basic strategy, the sooner a victim can change the attacker's mind and get them to realize that they've made a mistake, the more likely they are to abort the attack. In essence, your job is not necessarily to defeat and apprehend the attacker but rather to provide vigorous and aggressive defense, utilizing any object in your environment and applying the five principles of real world violence as we have previously discussed, to get them to realize they've made a mistake. i.e. the attack is harder than they thought which will trigger a shift to their own flight instinct and will likely cause them to abort.

Needless to say, the more training you do, the better you are going to be prepared to deal with this intense situation. We have found that with the thousands of females that we have trained over the years, many of them having been survivors of attacks, that they have often told us that even if they fought back – and this is a small minority of them – and they were still raped, they believe that they were able to recover quicker because in terms of their own mental state and consequential understanding, they had truly tried with all their might and resources to negate the situation.

Having said that, there are no absolutes. If you believe that passive cooperation is the only valid survival strategy, that is a call that you would have to make at that given time. No instructor or anybody else for that matter, could tell you when to cooperate or when to fight. However, one of the mistakes people often make is not realizing they're being attacked until it's too late. Therefore, if you're able to program your response ahead of time and know what you can and can't do, the chance of survival and stopping the attacker is significantly increased.

Now that we have discussed some of the threat issues, we will summarize below some basics in terms of personal safety on foot:

- Knowing where you're going is critically important. If you are lost and don't know where you are going, you are obviously distracted and an easier target.
- Showing you're actively aware by turning your head and looking around creates a significant deterrent value.
- Rationing your awareness and ensuring you're not distracted by being actively aware and not being on your cellphone or listening to music in areas or places that you are vulnerable is important.
- Minimizing your target attractiveness by making sure that you don't wear excessive jewelry or any other items that may cause

undue attention in environments that are not safe and secure is a critical action.

- Striving to control and protect your personal space, whilst not always possible, means that it is much harder for someone with ill-intent to take you by surprise.
- Lastly, preparation and the ability to fight or flight in their own right, becomes a significant skill set inclusion. Whilst there are numerous other things that are critical and could be applied, such as traveling in groups and planning the time of your travel, these sorts of things should, as a matter of course, become part of the way you plan as a whole.

In summarizing, some of these considerations, when it comes to personal safety, obviously the capability of being able to defend yourself, as we discussed previously in this book, should be a life skill that everybody attains (please reference chapters 1, 3 and 5 for more information). The level you want to take this too is totally up to you but I would wholeheartedly suggest that you attend some sort of realistic self-defense training to develop a basic skill level that you would hopefully never need. In addition, the health benefits alone make it a worthwhile endeavor even if the self-defense skills set was not the priority. Remember, ideally you should try and ensure that you match your level of security preparation with the threats you're likely to face, otherwise you would just become paranoid and not be able to enjoy life. If you are in an environment where active attackers, armed robberies and the like or some sort of high level threat is an ongoing concern, the more time, effort and energy you can put into preparing yourself and mitigating the threat, the better it is for you and your loved ones. If you are in an environment that is much safer, simply applying a few basics security measures may mean you do not have items stolen or just that you drive in a safer manner because you understand awareness and adrenal response.

Your virtual presence – cybercrime, digital crime and identity theft

The next issue that I would like to touch on are the ever-evolving area of cyber-crime, identity theft and/or identity fraud, all of which are ongoing realities that will become larger issues as our virtual lifestyles continue to develop. We need to remember that, whilst physical threat in terms of our work and personal life may seem to be obvious, most of us have another significant presence and life – that of our virtual persona. The issues around our virtual protection are evolving so quickly that it is hard to keep up. Emerging threats have yet have yet to be determined. The full extent of these problems are only being dealt with on a comparatively basic level by most people, but will need to improve significantly as threats expand and evolve. The reality, as previously discussed when we spoke about technology right at the beginning of this book (Chapter 1), means that because you can sit at home and engage with almost anyone in the world via social media, email or any other online tool, this makes you exceptionally vulnerable. Aspects, such as cyber-harassment, cyber-bullying and more conventional, cyber-theft or cyber-fraud can manifest in many ways. Some common approaches include stealing information off your laptop or PC by phishing, whereby people try and draw you in with an email or spoofing, whereby fake emails or fake websites are set up to gain your information or access to your system. The ever-present threats of viruses or malware attacking your system, are now commonplace realities.

You should strive to develop basic online protective practices and capabilities that safeguard your virtual lifestyle, just as you would hopefully try to protect your physical one. This topic is so large that it could take up several books in its own right but some basic guidelines and action items are listed below:

• You should not share personal or sensitive information online unless you absolutely must (in which case you really need to confident in the site you are using and who else has access to it) and you should be exceptionally careful about what you do share.

- Password safety and password security is critical. You should not choose simple passwords and you should change them often.
- Be careful what networks you connect too, the perception that WIFI is safe is not real and as long as you are on someone else's network, you are vulnerable.
- Remember to be savvy across all devices, not just your home or work computer, we tend to forget that our mobile devices are now computers in their own right and as we capitalize on cloud computing and cloud based data storage we need to remember that other people may be able to access whatever it is we store in the Cloud.
- Remember social media is an open platform. There is no such thing as online privacy and protection – if you share something it's out there!
- Monitor which APPs are collecting data and have location capabilities and minimize this wherever possible. As an example – even innocent Apps that may serve to locate your phone if lost may have a nefarious purpose for someone with ill intent who could track and follow you with ease.
- With the evolution of Social Media be very careful of Social Engineering which has reached new levels of epic risk exposure. Whilst social engineering tactics have been used successfully for decades to gain login information and access to encrypted files, it has never been easier nor more consequential than it is today.
- We control so few safety variables in Cyber space, so ensure that you maintain basic virus and firewall protection as a minimum. This includes ensuring that your security measures are kept up to date and current.
- Try and stay current to evolving threats such as new phishing emails so that you can make sure you do not get caught out. This issue is very important based on how quickly cyber crime is evolving.

Whilst the above is by no means an extensive list, these simple practices could mean the difference between somebody having enough information to steal from you and somebody not. While we're often bombarded with this sort of information, it's quite important that we make sure that we apply it and do not fall into the trap of being negligent or ignorant. As soon as we think it can't happen to us, we become very vulnerable.

If you think about what information may be on your laptop or home computer (or even your phone), it should be enough, if we're honest, for somebody to clone and steal your identity. This may not be as complex as we perceive because all an attacker really needs are some personal details… An emerging threat that proves the complexity of cyber risk is the evolving threat of cyber fraud mixed with identify theft and conventional crime. Let's examine an example to explain this.

Imagine you were taking a long-distance flight and somebody was able to get hold of your flight details and your next-of-kin contacts. They may contact your next-of-kin while you're on the flight and not reachable, and say that you've been hurt and they require a credit card to pay for hospital admission. They provide personal details and tell you that they will put a doctor on the phone – inevitably an accomplice. While in some cases this may not work as skeptical people may believe that there's no way this is real, however, in some cases people simply provide credit card information straight away because they think that it is real and feel that they better cooperate straight away to help their loved one. They feel that they just can't take the chance, since when they try to get a hold of you, your phone and other means of contact would not be accessible. Airlines are highly unlikely to give out details regarding passengers without their passengers' consent, which aids criminals in these sorts of crimes. This is just one example of a crime happening every day because people with ill intent can so easily get our information in the virtual world.

ATM crime and fraud

The example in the previous section should create some concern about what we share and what we don't, how we store our information and how accessible it may be. This is also true in the physical world with the need to be careful about documents you throw away or discard when they're not relevant is also important. If somebody could pick up a document, get a picture of you, your date of birth, your place of residence and potentially a credit card number, they may be able to transact or mimic you in numerous ways, which could have significant negative consequences.

Leading on from the basic overviews of cyber-crime and personal security is basic ATM and credit card security awareness. We should understand that ATM fraud is a massive industry. You should be really careful about which ATMs you use, how you select them and what you are doing while you're using the ATM. For example, if you are on the phone at the same time you are likely distracted and as such an easy target. In terms of safe practice some general guidelines you should take into account some of the following:

- You should be careful of the ATM you select based on its surroundings and the people there. By scanning the ATM before you approach you can be more aware of any threats before even considering using the ATM.
- You should always inspect the ATM to make sure that there are no additional devices, hidden cameras or other aspects that 'look like they don't belong'. If something looks wrong find another ATM.
- You should be especially careful of personal space. As secondary crimes such as pickpocketing are also common when people are focused on using the ATM in front of them.
- You should make sure that people are not shoulder surfing or looking at your password.
- You should never accept somebody providing you with advice or trying to assist you when you use an ATM, if you need help you should go into a bank.
- If you have any concerns, you should abort as soon as possible and notify the bank regarding your concern.

When it comes down to choosing an ATM, obviously one that's well-lit, with some people movement around it, in an environment that would be well protected should be your first choice. If you ever have the opportunity to use ATMs that are right outside a bank branch or within the bank, that should be your preference. In terms of credit card protection, remember that you should always keep your credit card in sight. If you have a pay wave technology (RFID) enabled card – which is the norm now, you should buy a protective sheath or ensure your wallet or purse has embedded RFID protection as its exceptionally easy for people to clone such cards. You should set transaction limits and be very careful what websites you are willing to provide your credit card details to.

Summary

Whilst the list of different threat actions and associated scenarios is large and the options available in response to each issue would require a book in their own right, this section serves to provide a generic over-view with regard to some of the more common issues. To sum up the key issues, you should remember that it is impossible to cover every possible scenario and that in fact, scenario responses to any given situation could probably also each take up their own book. We have covered just the basics of static, mobile and on foot security. We also looked at Cybercrime and ATM safety. Physical assault and personal self-defense have been the topics of thousands of books. I urge you to please view the bibliography and recommended reading section of this book for further reading in areas where you may want to learn more.

Bibliography and Recommended Reading

Ariely, D. (2008). *Predictably Irrational, The Hidden Forces that Shape our Decisions.* HarperCollins, Melbourne.

Ariely, D. (2012). *The Honest Truth About Dishonesty: How We Lie to Everyone—Especially Ourselves,* Harper Collins. New York.

ASIS Foundation. (2009). *Compendium of the ASIS Academic/Practitioner Symposium, 1997–2008.* http://www.asisonline.org/foundation/noframe/19972008_CompendiumofProceedingspdf. (Accessed: 15 December 2010).

ASIS International online library. (2015). http://www.asisonline.org/library/glossary/s.pdf. (Accessed: November 2015).

ASQA. (2013). http://www.asqa.gov.au/. (Accessed: 10 November 2015).

Asken, M., Grossman, D. and Christensen, L. (2010). Warrior Mindset: Mental toughness skills for a nations peacekeepers. Mildstat, IL: Warrior Science Publications.

Aveni, T. (2005). Critical Analysis of Contemporary Police Training. Paper presented at the State Bar of Texas 17th Annual Suing and Defending Government Entitles Course. San Antonio.

Ayoob, M. (2007). The Gun Digest Book of Combat Hand Gunnery. Iola, WI: Krause Publications.

Bandura, A. (1973). *Aggression: A social learning analysis.* Englewood Cliffs, NJ: Prentice Hall.

Ben-Asher, D. (1983). *Fighting Fit: The Israel Defence Forces guide to physical fitness and self-defence.* New York: Perigee books.

Ben-Keren, G. (2014). *Real World Solutions to Real World Violence.* Tuttle Publishing. VT.

Bratton, W. and Kelling, G. (2006). *There Are No Cracks in the Broken Windows: Ideological academics are trying to undermine a perfectly good idea.*

http://old.nationalreview.com/comment/bratton_kelling200602281015. asp. (Accessed: 10 January 2010).

Braunig, M. (1993). *The Executive Protection Bible.* Aspen, CO: ESI Education Development Organisation.

Calibre Press. (1987). *Surviving Edged Weapons.* Northbrook: Calibre Press Video Production.

Caplan, C. (1961). An approach to community mental health. New York, NY: Grune & Stratton.

Caplan, G. (1964). Principles of preventive psychiatry. New York, NY: Basic Book.

Consterdine, P. (1997). *Streetwise: The complete manual of personal security and self defence.* Leeds: Summersdale Press.

Cooper, J. (1989). *The Principles of Personal Defence.* Boulder, CO: Paladin Press.

De Becker, G. (1997). The Gift of Fear. New York: Dell Publishing.

De Nevers, R. (2009). Private Security Companies and the Laws of War. *Security Dialogue,* 40(2). New York: Sage Publications: 169–190.

Dictionary of the Social Sciences. (2007). *Broken Windows Theory.* Craig Calhoun (Ed.) 2002. Oxford: Oxford University Press.

Dror, I. (2007). Perception of Risk and the Decision to Use Force. Policing. Oxford: Oxford University Press: 265–272.

Dror, I., Busemeyer, J.R. and B, Basola. (1999). Decision making under time pressure: An independent test of sequential sampling models: Memory and cognition. 27(4): 713–725.

Elhanan, P. (1985). *Keep 'em alive the bodyguard's trade.* Boulder: Paladin Press

Flesch, R. (1994). *Defensive Tactics for Law Enforcement, Public Safety & Correction Officers.* Florida: Gould publications.

Graham, K. and Homel, R. (2008). *Raising the Bar: Preventing aggression in and around bars, pubs and clubs.* Cullompton, United Kingdom: Willan Publishing.

Grossman, D. (2009). *On Killing: The psychological cost of learning to kill in war and society. EBOOK.* New York: E-rights/E-reads Ltd Publishers.

Grossman, D. (2010). *Killology. www.killology.com. (Accessed: 1 February 2015).*

Grossman, D. and Christensen, L. (2008). *On Combat: The psychology and physiology of deadly conflicts in War and Peace.* Millstadt, IL: Warrior Science Publications.

Hammond, G.T. (2001). The Mind of War: John Boyd and American Security. Washington, D.C: Smithsonian Institution Press.

Hanover, D. (2008). Dennis Survival Jujitsu: Defeating Violence with Honor. Israel: Dennis Survival Jujitsu Foundation.

Hoel, H, Sparks, K. and Cooper, C. (2001). The cost of violence/stress at work and the benefits of a violence/stress-free working environment. Geneva: International Labor Organization (ILO).

Howe, P. (2005). Leadership and training for the fight. Indiana: Authorhouse.

Howe, P. (2009). The Tactical Trainer (Training for the fight). Indiana: Authorhouse.

International Firearm Training Academy (IFTA). (2009). Basic, Intermediate and Tactical use of Handgun, Shotgun and Rifle manuals. Krugersdorp: IFTA (Pty) Ltd.

International Foundation for Protection Officers. (1992). Protection Officer Training Manual. Stoneham, MA: Butterworth-Heinemann.

Kahneman, D. (2011). *Thinking Fast and Slow.* Farrar, Strauss and Giroux. New York.

King, J.A. (2001). *Providing Protective Services.* Shawnee mission: Varro press.

Kotwica, K. (2009). *2009 Security Budget Research Report: Impact of the Economic Downturn. USA: The Security Executive Council.*

Lieberman, M.D. (2013). *Social: Why our brains are wired to connect.* New York, NY: Crown.

Linstead, S. (1997). *Abjection and Organization: Men, violence, and management. Human Relations,* 50(9). September: Wollongong, NSW: The Tavistick Institute.

Maslow, A. (1943). A Theory of Human Motivation, *Psychological Review,* 50(4): 370–96. New York: Philosophical Library.

Marrs, J. (2009). Developing the Warrior Mind: Boyd's OODA loop and Cooper's Color Code lay the foundation. http://www.spartancops.com/developing-warrior-mind-boyds-ooda-loop-coopers-color-code-lay-foundation/. (Accessed: 10 February 2011).

Mead-Niblo, D. (1995). *Security in the Hospitality Industry.* PhD Dissertation. Melbourne: The University of Melbourne.

Maslow, A. (1943). A Theory of Human Motivation, *Psychological Review,* 50(4): 370–96. New York: Philosophical Library.

Minnaar, A. (1997). *Partnership Policing between the South African Police Service and the South African Private Security Industry.* (Information document prepared for National Policy & Strategy, Division: Management Services, SAPS.) SAPS Research Centre, Pretoria. June.

Minnaar, A. (2004). *Inaugural Lecture: Private-public partnerships: Private security, crime prevention and policing in South Africa*. Florida: Department of Security Risk Management, School of Criminal Justice, College of Law, University of South Africa.

Minnaar, A. (2005). Private-public partnerships: Private security, crime prevention and policing in South Africa. *Acta Criminologica: Southern African Journal of Criminology*. 18(1): 85–114.

Minnaar, A. (2006). A comparative review of the regulating of the private security industries in South Africa, Australia and the United Kingdom (UK). Paper presented to the 6th Biennial International Criminal Justice Conference: *Policing in Central and Eastern Europe-Past, present and futures*. Ljubljana, Slovenia. 21–23 September 2006.

Minnaar, A. (2007a). Oversight and monitoring of non-state/private policing: The private security practitioners in South Africa. In: S. Gumedze, (Ed.). 2007. *Private security in Africa: Manifestation, challenges and regulation*. Institute for Security Studies: Brooklyn, Tshwane. ISS Monograph No. 139: 127–149.

Minnaar, A. (with a contribution by K. Pillay). (2007b). *A review of the issues and challenges facing the private security industry in South Africa*. Unpublished research report. Department of Security Risk Management, University of South Africa/Open Society Foundation Society-South Africa.

Minnaar, A. and Ngoveni, P. (2004). The relationship between the South African Police Service and the private security industry: Any role for outsourcing in the prevention of crime? *Acta Criminologica: Southern African Journal of Criminology*. 17(1): 42–65.

Mroz, R. (2003). Tactical Defensive Training for Real-Life Encounters: Practical self-preservation for Law Enforcement. Boulder Colorado: Paladin Press.

Newman, O. (1972). Defensible Space: Crime Prevention Through Urban Design. New York: Macmillan.

Passfield, N. and Schneider, G. (2015). The multiplex view to Hard Risk Management – time for another dimension. *Risk Management Today*, Vol 25 No 6. Lexis Nexis: 96–99.

Schneider, G. (2005). *An examination of the required operational skills and training standards for a Close Protection Operative in South Africa*. MTech Dissertation. Pretoria: University of South Africa.

Schneider, G. (2009). Know your enemy – the importance of a threat assessment. *Security Focus – The official industry journal for professional risk practitioners: Security, Safety, Health, Environment and Quality Assurance. January Edition.* Security Publications, South Africa: 50.

Schneider, G. (2009). High Risk Close Protection. *Security Focus – The official industry journal for professional risk practitioners: Security, Safety, Health, Environment and Quality Assurance. April Edition.* Security Publications, South Africa: 47.

Schneider, G. (2009). *Beyond the Bodyguard: Proven tactics and dynamic strategies for protective practice success.* Boca Raton, USA: Universal Publishers.

Schneider, G. (2012). *The design and development of the Practical Use of Force Training Model for the private security industry.* Doctoral Thesis. Pretoria: University of South Africa.

Schneider G. (2012). *Close Personal Protection in Action: An analysis of the evacuation of Prime Minister Julia Gillard on Australia day 2012*: Asia Pacific Security Magazine April/May, My Security Media Pty Ltd: 47–49.

Schneider G. (2012). An Eyes Wide Open Approach in Africa. *Asia Pacific Security Magazine,* June/July, My Security Media Pty Ltd: 8–10.

Schneider G. (2013). The Security Safety Cross Over: How Wide is the Gap. *Asia Pacific Security Magazine*, Issue 45, My Security Media Pty Ltd: 30–31.

Schneider, G. and Minnaar, A. (2013). Business case for safety and security. *Security Focus. The official industry journal for professional risk practitioners: Security, Safety, Health, Environment and Quality Assurance.* Vol 31 No 10. Security Publications, South Africa: 18–20.

Schneider, G. (2015). Business in Emerging Markets – An eyes wide open approach. *Risk Management Today,* Vol 25 No 3. Lexis Nexis: 48–50.

Schneider G. (2015). Security and Risk Management, the next level. *Asia PacificSecurity Magazine*, Issue 45, My Security Media Pty Ltd: 24–25.

Schneider G. (2015). Security and Risk Management, the next level. *Chief IT Magazine*, Spring 2015 Issue, My Security Media Pty Ltd: 30–31.

Schneider, D. and Down, K. (2016). Dynamic Risk Equilibrium – The next wave. *Risk Management Today,* Vol 26 No 10. Lexis Nexis: 180–184.

Standards Australia. (2009). *AS/NZS ISO 31000:2009 Risk management—Principles and guidelines.*

Standards Australia. (2010). *Handbook 327: 2010 Communicating and Consulting about Risk.*

Stoddard, A., Harmer, A. and DiDomenico, V. (2008). *The Use of Private Security Providers and Services in Humanitarian Operations.* London: Humanitarian Policy Group.

Strom, K., Berzofsky, M., Shook-sa, B., Barrik, K., Daye, C., Horsteman, N. and Kinsey, S. (2010). *The Private Security Industry: A Review of the Definitions, Available Data Sources, and Paths Moving Forward.* Bureau of Justice Statistics. USA: RTI International.

Swanton, B. (1993). Police and Private Security: Possible Directions. *Trends and Issues in Crime and Criminal Justice,* 42. Canberra: Australian Institute of Criminology.

Swiss Confederation. (2010). *International Code of Conduct for Private Security Providers.* Montreux: Swiss Government.

Tedeschi, J. and Felson, R. (1994). Violence, Aggression, and Coercive Actions. Washington, DC: American Psychological Association.

Thompson, G. (1999). Dead or Alive. London: Summersdale Press.

Thompson, G. (1999a). Fear the friend of exceptional people. London: Summerdale press.

Thompson, L. (2003). The bodyguard manual: Protection techniques of the professionals. London: Greenhill books.

Tuckey, M. (2004). *National Guidelines for Incident Management, Conflict Resolution and Use of Force.* South Australia: Australian Centre for Policing Research.

Winlow. S., Hobbs, D., Lister, S. and Hadfield, P. (2001). Get Ready to Duck: Bouncers and the realities of ethnographic research on violent groups. *British Journal of Criminology* 4: 536–548. United Kingdom: The Academic Research Library.

About the Author

D r. Gavriel (Gav) Schneider CPP, FIS (SA), FAIM, FGIA, AARPI, MAIPIO.

Dr. Gav is an acknowledged leader in the field of human based risk management and the psychology of risk, He is a serial entrepreneur and has been running his own businesses since 2001. He has conducted business in over 17 countries and provided a wide range of services for a very diverse client base ranging from heads of state to school teachers. He is a leading academic in his field and is a much-sought after International speaker. Gav has over 2 decades of experience managing various aspects of Risk (Strategic Risk, Safety, Emergency Response, and Intelligence), specialising in security risk management. He is a highly-experienced bodyguard and close protection expert and holds a 7th degree Black Belt in Krav Maga and Jujitsu. He is an inducted member of the South African Martial Arts Hall of Fame and is listed in the Israeli Museum of Martial Arts History for his contributions. Along with a Doctorate in Criminology, and a Master's Degree in Security Risk Management, he holds an extensive list of additional qualifications and is a Fellow of the South African Institute of Security, A Fellow of the Governance Institute of Australia and a Fellow of the Australian Institute of Management. Gav has trained thousands of people in his own right, and his companies have trained close to 150,000 people in many countries.

CPSIA information can be obtained
at www.ICGtesting.com
Printed in the USA
BVHW03s1213190518
516743BV00021B/181/P